Richard Gardiner

Memoirs if the Life and Writings of Richard Gardiner

Richard Gardiner

Memoirs if the Life and Writings of Richard Gardiner

ISBN/EAN: 9783744685603

Printed in Europe, USA, Canada, Australia, Japan

Cover: Foto ©Thomas Meinert / pixelio.de

More available books at **www.hansebooks.com**

MEMOIRS

OF THE

LIFE and WRITINGS

(PROSE AND VERSE)

OF

R-ch--d G-rd-n-r, Efq.

Alias

DICK MERRY-FELLOW,

Of Serious and Facetious Memory!

AUTHOR of

The HISTORY *of* PUDICA;	*The* CONTEST;
An ELEGY *on the death of Lady Afgill*;	LETTERS *to Sir* H— H—, *and* T— W— C—, *Efq*.
An EXPEDITION *to the Weft-Indias*;	*A* FRAGMENT;
The LYNN MAGAZINE;	*The* TRIPPING-JURY; NAVAL-REGISTER, &c.

" A man who has *much* WIT, but *too little* DISCRETION ; one
" who has TALENTS fufficient to adorn the *beft* fubjects,
" and to give fome confequence even to the *worft*; but
" who has (except in a few cafes) been fo unfortunate in his
" choice of SUBJECTS, that our *fmiles* are frequently mixed
" with *pain*, and our *admiration* with *difguft*."

CHARACTER, 1768.

LONDON:

Printed for G. KEARSLY, Fleet-ftreet; and M. BOOTH,
NORWICH.

January 1, 1782.

P R E L U D I O.

LEST the abilities and character of this Gentleman should suffer by an improper application of his juvenile and adult performances, whether satirical or political, to the purposes of malice or party, we are induced, from the purest motives, and in justice to his memory, to offer the following account of his LIFE and WRITINGS, which we

are

are enabled to do from the moſt in-
diſputable authorities, to wit, *his
own compoſitions*, and which, we can
aſſure the public, *were intended by
himſelf for the preſs.*

TRUTH being the fureſt teſt of
compilation, we ſhall, without any
prejudice ariſing from hope or fear,
opinion or party, give a faithful, if
not a comprehenſive, narrative of
ſuch circumſtances as come ſafely
within our knowledge, in doing
which, we ſhall adopt that excellent
line of Shakeſpeare's.

Nothing extenuate nor ſet down aught in malice.

As he choſe to give himſelf the ap-
pellation of DICK MERRY-FELLOW
in a well-known publication *, we

---

* PUDICA.

think

think ourfelves fully warranted in now applying it; and it is hoped, that as the following fheets were rather *haftily got up*, to ufe a theatric expreffion, the Public will readily excufe a want of method, or of ftile.

Eft brevitate opus, ut currat fententia, neu fe Impediat verbis laffas onerantibus aures:

HOR.

I write, as I would talk; am fhort, and clear;
Not clog'd with words, that load the weari'd ear.

WE have, in moft inftances, thought proper to blank the names of perfons; not becaufe we wanted confidence to infert them at length, but becaufe we would avoid giving offence. To thofe already acquainted with our hero's tranfactions, the omiffion will be fufficiently underftood, and to thofe who are not---it

is

is immaterial. An anonymous ſtory is as entertaining, and as inſtructive, as if authorized by the greateſt name.

It may be aſked, Who are we? we are indefinite! and therefore reſtrained, by the firſt problem of *Euclid*,---to no point. Beſides, *memoirs* are of the plural---and ſo are we!

MEMOIRS

OF THE

LIFE and WRITINGS

OF

R-ch--d G--d-n-r, Efq.

Alias

DICK MERRY-FELLOW.

THE GENTLEMAN, whofe Pofthumous Effays we have taken fome pains to collect, was fo eminently diftinguifhed by his learning, wit, and fatire, that his writings need not the force of elogy to recommend them to public notice.

Dicere verum Quid vetat ?

HE was born at Saffron-Walden in Effex, October 4, 1723; and died at Mount-Amelia in the parifh of Ingoldifthorpe and county of Norfolk, on Friday, September 14, 1781, aged juft fifty-feven years, eleven months, and ten days.

B   HIS

His father was a fon of John G—d-n-r, Efq. of Aldborough-Hall near Aldborough in the county of Suffolk, who was a Captain in Lord Cutt's regiment of foot, and died at Minorca, in the reign of Queen Anne, *Anno Dni.* 1708, when that ifland fell a conqueft to the Britifh troops, and fquadron under the command of Admiral Sir John Leake, and General Stanhope.

He was a man of confiderable property and eftate, and of fuch influence in the borough of Aldborough (then a populous and flourifhing fea-port town, though in this prefent age great part of it has been fwallowed up by the Britifh ocean that wafhes the eaft fide of the borough) that on his recommendation, the reprefentatives for Aldborough were generally chofen, an honour that he declined himfelf, as his military duty (being Captain of foot in Lord Cutt's regiment) fo frequently called him into foreign fervice.

He died at an early period of life, but had this compenfation for the fhortnefs of it, that he lived and ferved his country in an age of heroes, and partook of the glories of that immortal reign, and of the important victories acquired by the all-conquering arms of Prince Eugene and the Duke of Marleborough. Though happy in an honourable death himfelf, in the fervice of his country, yet it was an irreparable lofs in every

refpeƈt

refpect to his fon (the late Dr. G——) who was then an infant of fix years old, by whofe premature deceafe, became not only a minor, but an orphan, his mother being dead before. The lofs of both parents at fuch an age, can only be felt by thofe who have fortunately lived to experience the tendernefs of parents till the time of manhood. How frequently do we fee the fortune, property and profperity of a family, fall into ruin, where the protecting care of a fond, indulgent, and confiderate father is wanting to fupport it!

His father, the late Rev. JOHN G—D-N-R, LL. D. was born in the firft year of Queen Anne, *Anno Dni.* 1702. In 1729, he was prefented to the rectory of Brunftead in the hundred of Happing and County of Norfolk, by the right honourable William Neville, Lord Abergavenny; and in the year 1731, he was licenced Rector, or perpetual Curate, of St. Giles, in the patronage of the Dean and Chapter, and Curate of St. Gregory, both in the city of Norwich.

In the faid year, 1731, he was prefented to the valuable rectory of Maffingham *Magna* St. Mary's with All Saints, by that munificent patron, Sir Robert Walpole, knight of the garter, firft lord-commiffioner of the Treafury, and prime minifter to George I. and II. univerfally acknowledged the greateft ftatefman of the age he lived in.

H₅

HE was Doctor of Laws in the Univerfity of Cambridge, and domeftic Chaplain to the Earl of Orford. Sir William Yonge, in a copy of verfes which he wrote, November 17, 1731, and fent to Lady Orford, then on a vifit at the feat of Sir Henry Bedingfield at Oxburgh-Hall, while the noble Earl was entertaining his illuftrious friends at Houghton; he mentions the worthy Doctor amongft the other guefts in the follow-ing lines:

" Next G—D-N-R, Chaplain to our hoft,
" A model for all priefts to boaft ;
" Whom WALPOLE loves, as far politer,
" Than thofe grim *Rooks*, who wear the *Mitre.*"

DR. G—D-N-R was married October 6, 1722, to a daughter of JOHN TURNER, Efq. of Saffron-Walden in the county of Effex. She died at Great Maffingham, October 10, 1759.

. THE Doctor lived the much-refpected rector of this church near forty years, until the 15th of November, 1770, when, to the unfpeakable grief of his family and friends, he departed this life, *Ætat.* 68.

HIS remains were interred in the chancel of Great Maffingham, by the altar, next to the grave. of his late affectionate wife, and tender parent to her children.

HIS

His pall was fupported by fix of the neigh-
bouring clergy, whofe concern in that laft melancholy office, was alone exceeded by the poignant
feelings of thofe more nearly allied.

Over the grave-ftone, near the altar, is the
following infcription :

H. S. E.

JOHANNES GARDINER,

L L. D.

Per triginta annos

et Amplius

Hujus Ecclefiæ

RECTOR.

The foregoing was found after his deceafe, in
his own hand writing, and was therefore put
upon the ftone in preference to any other infcription.

Ob. Novem. 15 *Die* 1770, *ætat.* 68.

Lapidam

Clariffimo Patri

Ricardus Filius Superftes

Marens Pofuit.

MDCCLXXI.

A hatchment is over the grave-ftone, with the
arms of Gardiner and Turner.

The

THE late Dr. G—D-N-R was a man univerfally refpeſted throughout life; a man of learning, and a gentleman: his excellent difcourfes in the pulpit proclaimed him to be the firſt; his addrefs and affability out of it, to be the laſt.

> With fpirit, eafe, and elegance to tell
> The rules for judging and for aſting well.

HE was a moſt tender parent to his children, an affectionate hufband; a humane man to all! the tears of his parifhioners at his funeral, bore an honourable teſtimony of his virtues.

HE, like his father, was univerfally eſteemed and perfonally beloved wherever he refided: this is no flattery, but juſtice to his memory; his many charitable aſts endeared him to the poor; his eafy and friendly deportment to the rich, and his ſtriſt attention to his paſtoral and religious duties, acquired him the refpeſt of all.

> *Vivit poſt Funera Virtus.*

HIS children followed the military profeffion of their grandfather: he lived to furvive two of his fons, who died in the fervice of their country; and the fame military fpirit defcended to his grandchildren, one of whom was killed in America, and two now remain in the army.

> " Their grandfire's trufty fword they long'd to wield,
> " While guns, drums, trumpets, call them to the field.

DR.

Dr. G—d-n-r had, by ——— Turner, his wife, many children, of whom only four lived to the age of twenty-one years, and of which two only furvived their much-lamented parents.

1. Richard, of whom we have to fpeak more at large.

2. John, who died at fea, in the command of the Bedford man of war of feventy guns, and was buried off the Rock of Lifbon, February 8, 1747.

3. William, who ferved with his eldeft bro-ther at the fiege of Guadelupe, in the Weft In-dies, and was Lieutenant of the 4th regiment of foot : he died at fea, on his paffage home from the Englifh garrifon in the citadel of Baffe-Terre, Guadelupe, and was buired off the ifland of St. Kitt's, in July 1761.

4. Margaret, married to the Rev. Thomas Money, Rector of Bracon-Afh in Norfolk, and of Stratford in Suffolk, by whom fhe had two fons, both in the fervice; Thomas the eldeft, born Oct. 16, 1752, now a Captain in the 69th regiment em-ployed in the Weft Indies, and lately on the con-queft of St. Euftatia, one of the Carribbee iflands belonging to the Dutch : the fecond fon, John, named after his grandfather Dr. John G—d-n-r, born December 8, 1756, was a Lieutenant in the

63d

63d regiment, and Aid-de-camp to Earl Cornwallis, commander in chief of the Britifh forces in South Carolina. He was employed in the army from the age of 16 years, and ferved with reputation during the whole of the prefent unfortun te war in America, where his inconfolable parents and lamenting fri nds had the misfortune to lofe him, gallantly fighting at the head of the 63d regiment and a derachment from the army, which was fent by Lord Cornwallis, to lead into action againft fuperior forces, commanded by an American General at Black-Stocks in South Carolina, November 9, 1780.

O meek-ey'd Peace! refume thy golden reign,
And waft thy blessings o'er th' Atlantic main.

HE was efteemed an exceeding good officer for his years, and promifed fair to rife to great emplovments in the army. Earl Cornwallis made honourable mention of him in his official difpatches to the Secretary of State, and feemed to lament the lofs with a concern almoft equal to that of his neareft friends and family-connections. He died of his wounds, November 15, a few days after the action, *ætat.* 24.

THE following infcription was wrote to his memory, by RICHARD GARDINER, Efq. of Mount Amelia in the County of Norfolk.

To

[9]

To the MEMORY of

LIEUTENANT JOHN MONEY,

Aid de Camp to Earl Cornwallis, who at the age
of 24, was killed at the head of the 63d regiment, ngaged againſt fuperior numbers, at
Black-Stocks, in South Carolina, on the attack and defeat of General Sumpter, an
American General, November 9, 1780.

Freſh bloom the laurel by the ſword acquir'd,
Brave, gallant youth! with love of glory fir'd !
For thee *Cornwallis* weeps, tho' on his brow
Fair vict'ry ſmiles, and tears in conqueſt flow :
O ! early loſt ! who envies not thy fame
And death, that gives to thee a deathlefs name ?
Thy hardy vet'rans oft in danger tried,
Point penſive to the field where MONEY died :
Where, as he ſaw thee bleeding on the ground,
The rapid *Tarleton* paus'd, and clos'd thy wound.

TREMBLE, BRITANNIA's FOES ! let the proud *Gaul*,
And prouder *Spaniard* dread a mighty fall;
So young in arms when *Britons* veng'ance pour,
And finiſh'd heroes die at TWENTY-FOUR !

RICHARD G—D-N-R, Eſq. *alias* DICK MERRY-
FELLOW, was born at Saffron-Walden in the
county of Effex, October 4, 1723. He was
educated at Eton College, and afterwards became a member of the Univerſity of Cambridge,
where he was ſtudent for ſome years at Catherine-

Hall

Hall: during his refidence there, he was appointed to write the *tripofberfes*, as they are called, for the fenior proctor's exercife, upon the Pythagorean queftion of the *metempfychofis*, or the tranfmigration of fouls, which, as it is a fubject lately ftarted to the public, may perhaps not be unentertaining, or unworthy the attention of the learned reader.

Recte Statuit *Pythagoras* De METEMPSYCHOSI.

QUOS fubeat refoluta vicés, quæ regna pererret
Sofpes ab exequijs ANIMÆ, aut quæ tarda revifat
Corpora, non longum manfura, volatilis hofpes,
Hinc canere incipiam; nec tu. Indignere vocanti
PAN, deus Arcadiæ, et petulantia Numina FAUNI,
Quâcunque in formâ, quocunque fub ore latentes:
Quodque tenet Sylvas, varium et mutabile femper,
Quodque tenet fluvios: PROTEU VERTUMNE, puellæ
Ipfe anus infidians: tuque, O! DAPHNEIA LAURUS,
Da foliâ indulgens manibus carpenda Pudicis
Virgineos, heu! iam non virgo, oblita timores.

Ac veluti E Lento furgunt fimulaera metallo
Quæ Faber excudens vivos imitamine vultus
Evocat, ILLA ducem victorem fpirat imago,
Mollior HÆC cythereæ oculos rifufque folutos
Exprimit, aut lique facta volens facilifque fequetus;
Artifici ducente, alias fubitura figuras:
Sic varijs ANIMA, æthereo confifa vigori,
Ludit imaginibus, larvafque exuta priores
Mille vices patitur: videas modo cornua TAURI
Torquere, indomitum modo ad arma urgere LEONEM:

Nunc

Nunc magis innocuos alijs animalibus ignes
Infpirans multo circum blanditur amore :
Hinc CANIS exquiris cæcos fuper afpera greffus
Fida regens domino veftigia, pectoris ardor
Jam furis, et notos teftatur confcia vultus
Lingua, fimul corpufque pedefque et cauda rotantur :
Hinc juga paftorem fuper, aut in amæna locorum
Lanigeræ comitantur OVES, vocemque fequuntur :
Hinc celeres agitat pennas lapfura COLUMBA
In nemus umbri ferum, conjux ubi murmure noto
Refpondet curis, æquatque fidelis amorem.

    Nec tamen intereà naturas mobilis hofpes
Quaflibet induitur paffim et difcrimine nullo :
Ipfa EADEM affectus de corporis haurit EOSDEM
Relliquijs, adèo non vitæ oblita prioris :
Ipfa fiti conftans femper, femperque fidelis
Antiquos fervat verfà fub imagine mores.

    Hinc ratione regi quâdem, rerumque fagaci
Notitiâ caltere FERÆ, et fapere alta videntur :
Admirandum adèo quid habet folertia VULPIS ?
Aut LEPORIS ? querimur quid tardum ad retia PIS-
    CEM ?
Scit bene uterque dolos hominum : quid odora ca-
    num vis
Poffet, ab exactis olim raminifcitur annis
Cautum animal : temidoque eadem hinc aftutia pifci
Vitare æratos, quos fæpe tetenderat, hamos.

    Scilicet humano refoluta E Corpore prifcas
Affectat vires ANIMA, atque obftantia pennis
Clauftra pati indignans, veteres tentare volatus
Audet, et inceptos, quondem renovare labores :
                                        Corporis

Corpóreis iterum moderari fenfibus ardet
Arbitrio imperiofa fuo, SOLIUMQUE priori
Afcendit faftu, RERUMQUE EXQUIRIT HABENAS.

Quis tamen expediat 'fando quos lubrica formes
Induat, et miris ludat lafciva figuris ?
Quæ circum gracilis fufpendit ARANEA telas
Educens multo fubtilia fila labore,
Hæc olim SOPHUS emicuit fuper ardua cœli,
Quem raptavit amor : depictæ in limite chartœ
Monftravit SOLISQUE vias LUNÆ que meatus.
Vix memor ipfe fui ! duræ inclementia noctis
Abftulit incautum, atque opera imperfecta reliquit :
Hinc prifces iterum exercet non fignior artes
Pendula de tigno, aut fcanderas laquearia tecti
Defignat varios miro fubtemine gyros :
Hæc inter forfàn in juvet evafifle laborem
Humanum, aut veteris repectens vefligia vitæ
Angat fe defiderio, indoleatque recordens.

En ! tacits quœ cuncta notat labentia cælo
Sidera, quæ ventos et quæ prœnuntiat æftus
CORNIX !——PARTRIGIUS docuit qui plurima vates
IDEM erat, annofique habitans penetralia tecti-
VENDIDIT hic AURO pluvias folefque benignos
Naturæ leges figens pretio atque refigens :
Ipfa tamen propium fervat natura tenorem,
Et pluvias HOMO qui cecinit, canit improba CORNIX.

Quas pofthàc tamen ad fedes ille * AUREUS ORDO
Migrabit INOCNUM, tua fpes † MUSGROVA, tuæque

---

* The fellow-commoners, whofe proper habit is laced with gold tufts.
† Two celebrated beauties at Cambridge, 1742-3.—Mifs Mufgrave, and Mifs Hargrave.

Deliciæ

Deliciæ, HARGRAVIA, aut quæ fe fub corpora condet?
Non illum SOPHIÆ documenta, aut cura TOGATI
Exercet damnofa, nec hæc in prælia venit:
Sed teftivus AMOR, ftudij fed nefcia vita
Plena voluptatum variarum, atque otia libris
Sepofitis, RISUS, SUSPERIA, CARMINA CANTUS
——O ! paulum æthereâ TRITONIÆ defpice fede
Vidiftin CYTHEREA tuas invafit ATHENAS
Optavitque locūm regno, fociofque dicavit
Hos JUVENES :—at tu nê fævi, MAXIMA PALLAS,
Difcedens, numerum explebunt, ftudijfque minutis
Reddentur : quandem hos MUSCARUM augere cohortes
Cernere erit, fufofve examine PAPILIONUM :
Nec tum etiam furiæ veteres, flammaque fideles
Deftituent animas, fed plurima MUSCA priores
Dulce minifterium ! circum volitabit amicos :
Illa, PUELLARES venient quacunque catervæ
TOTA INHIANS folitos aget officiofa triumphos
Incidens capiti, aut libratis acre pennis
Mille dabit rofcis, IAM LIBERA, bafia labris.

Aft ubi funereæ rapient VERNONA forores
Totaque communi perfufa BRITANNIA luctu
Condet honorato quicquid mortale fepulchro :
Ille AQUILA aerios tentans fuper aftra volatus,
Contemptis nemorum alitibus, terrâque relictâ
Carpet iter fublime, deoque favente, CORUSCO
SUBSIDET SOLIO, atque iterum reget Arma TON-
ANTIS.

In comitijs prioribus Feb. 17, 1742-3.
RICARDUS GARDINER.
Aul. St. Cath. Cant. Alum.

At

AT what time, or in what manner, DICK MERRY-FELLOW left the Univerſity of Cambridge we are not told; but immagine it to be ſoon after the date of the above, Feb. 17, 1743; for we find him in 1748, " returned to Norwich, after having been abroad for *ſeveral* years."

HE had *then* made a campaign or two in Flanders, and, as the country people term it; travelled a good deal *to ſee foreign parts* ; but from a continued ſeries of misfortunes and diſappointments, finding little probability of ſucceeding in the *army*, he began to liſten to ſome propoſals of entering into the *church :* theſe had often been made to him, but he as often refuſed, generally giving for anſwer, " that he thought himſelf by " no means qualified for ſuch an undertaking," and called to mind the anſwer of Dr. Donne (afterwards Dean of St. Paul's) which he is ſaid to have made to Morton, Biſhop of Durham, who ſtrongly preſſed him to go into orders, " that ſome former irregularities * of his life " had been too notorious not to expoſe him to " the cenſure of the world, and perhaps bring " diſhonour to the ſacred funétion."

---

* The Doćtor having been abroad, in the expedition of the Earl of Eſſex againſt Cadiz, and at the Azore Iſlands, and reſided ſeveral years in Spain and Italy.

HE

HE continued in this refolution till the year 1748, when, having been taken prifoner at fea by a privateer, and thereby prevented joining the army as a *volunteer*, which was then affembled near Maeftricht, under the command of his Royal Highnefs the Duke of Cumberland, who was equally remarkable for rewarding his volunteers, as well as leading them to action;—being plundered by the French feamen, ftript of all his cloaths, carried to Dunkirk and put into the common jail there; returning to England from his confinement, and in this fituation, now fully convinced that fortune was not his friend, and the conclufion of the peace following the year after (Oct. 18, 1748) he no longer hefitated to comply with the repeated inftances of his friends, and accordingly entered into Deacon's orders, in which he continued but a very little while, and further than which, he never proceeded in the church.

From brown to black,—to red,—to black by rote,
And, lobfter-like, from black to red turns coat.

To the church he had fome pretentions, having had his education at an Univerfity, from whence he brought away fome *Latin* and *Greek*, though not a great deal of either.

As to *divinity matters*, if not a perfect ftranger to them, he was, however, fo little fufpected of having made any great acquaintance there, that

is

it was a common queſtion with his intimate
friends to aſk, " whether the Biſhop, who gave
" him his orders, examined him in the *Bible*, or
" in *Bland's Military Diſcipline.*"

Upon his return to Norwich, he ſtood the
banter of his companions for ſome time, being
daily told " how well he became the *ſables*,—
" that Japan had not altered him for the worſe,
" and what a pity it was, black cloaths were only
" wore in mourning, ſome people looked ſo well
" in them." This laſt being always attended
with a concern for the relation * he had loſt,
which it was to be hoped was no near one; each
in his turn verifying the obſervation of *Horace.*

———————— *dummodo riſum*
Excutiat ſibi, non hic cuiquam parcit amico.

Dick Merry-fellow was now in the twenty-
fixth year of his age; and as the reader may expect ſome deſcription of him and his perſon, at
that period of life, we ſhall give it in as few
words as we can.

. He was not the *ingenui vultûs puer, ingenuique
pudoris* of the Latins, nor the *jeune Homme d'Eſprit*
of the French, though not remarkably deficient

* This was his brother John, who died at ſea and was
buried off the Rock of Liſbon, February 8, 1747.

in

in either figure or fenfe; he was far from being *genteel*, yet, as he had been ufed to a great deal of company, was not very *awkward*; his friends never thought him a *fool*, though he was feldom heard to fay any thing *very clever*, and when he did, it was always attended with a laugh from *himfelf firft.*

His perfon was rather tall and thin, his legs long and flender; the latter were often fubjects of ridicule amongft his acquaintance; and to fay the truth, were but *two poor fticks* indeed: his hair was of a colour that was a favourite of the *antients*, though we cannot fay the *moderns* have tafte enough to admire it; it was by them efteemed a mark of beauty; *Homer's* Helen was a Χρυσοκόμη, and the *Aurea Cæfaries* and *Flavi Capilli* amongft the Romans, ever mentioned with refpect, and applied to *admired* men and women, are inftances too well known to be repeated here; indeed *Horace* has faid fomething in praife of black hair and black eyes,

Spectandum nigris Oculis nigroque Capillo,

—But *he* might be a man of a *particular* fancy, and there's no accounting for that.

His complexion was fair, and he wanted not to be told of it, being very fond of his own *pretty* face, and often laughed at by his friends

for

for running up to *a glass* as soon as he came into
a room.

" Shine out bright sun, 'til I have brought a glass,
" That I may view my shadow as I pass."

As to his dress, in which, though confined to
the same colours, he contrived to *distinguish* him-
self from his reverend brethren, * and by the
help of a good quantity of powder, and not
wearing a shirt above *three days*, was generally
smarter than the rest of them ; and this gained
him no good-will among the graver sort, who was
used to make a great joke of his *spruce* coat,
and *plaistered* curls, and were often heard to say,
" what a *jessamy* parson we have got among us !
" a pretty *sprig* of divinity this !" with other
expressions of *severe wit* and *humour*,—talents the
clergy are generally found to excel in.

> At once the soft contagion seiz'd his breast,
> For what can Love's almighty pow'r controul ?
> The ruling passion ev'ry thought possest,
> And ev'ry fond idea fill'd his soul !

---

* Had *Dick* figured in the present age of *canonical foppery*, he
would not have been so much distinguished from his Reverend
brethren.

> Life, soul, and all, would claim th' attention less ;
> For life and soul is center'd all—in dress.
> *Non sic incerto mutantur flamine Syrtes,*
> *Nec folia hyberno jam tremefacta Noto.* PROPERT.

It

IT was at this memorable æra that DICK
MERRY-FELLOW made love to PUDICA, a young
lady of birth and great fortune, who he fondly
imagined had difcovered a *penchant* for him.

Ye fongs, fhells, philters, amulets, and charms,
Bring, quickly bring, PUDICA to my arms.

HE was naturally very vain, and miftook thofe
civilities which his character and appearance
might claim of any lady, for a partiality towards
him.

Is fhe a Woman ?—if a woman—then
My title's good—women were made for men.

THUS flattered into a perfect fecurity of being
poffeffed of an amiable confort, and a princely
revenue, he went on in the delirium of breath-
ing a *golden age*; it is not at all wonderful that
the moft poignant fenfations of vexation and diflike operated ftrongly, when the delufive phantom vanifhed on the bare word ECLAIRCISSE-
MENT.

CASTLES

CASTLES *in the* AIR:
A TALE.

THEY, who content on earth to ftay,
  To earth their views confine;
With rapture —— —— will furvey
  This Paradife of thine!

I, too, my willing voice would raife,]
  And equal rapture fhew;
But that the fceaes which others praife,
  For me are much *too low!*

I grant the hills are crown'd with trees,
  I grant the fields are fair;
But, after all, one nothing fees
  But what is *really there!*

True tafte ideal profpects feigns,
  Whilft on poetic wings,
'Bove earth, and all that earth contains,
  Unbounded fancy fprings!

To dwell on earth, grofs element,
  Let grovelling fpirits bear;
But I on nobler plans intent,
  Build *Caftles in the Air!*

No neighbour there can difagree,
  Or thwart what I defign;
For there, not only all I fee,
  But all I wifh, is mine!

No furly *landlord's* leave I want,
  To make or pull down fences;
I build, I furnifh, drain, and plant,
  Regardlefs of expences!

One

One thing, 'tis true, excites my fear,
　Nor let it feem furprifing ;
Whilft minifters from year to year,
　New taxes are devifing.

Left, earth being tax'd, as foon it may,
　Beyond what earth can bear ;
Our *Financier* a tax fhould lay
　— On *Cafles in the Air!*

Well with the end the means would fuit,
　Would he, in thefe our days,
Ideal plans to execute,
　Ideal taxes raife !

THINGS were in the moft favourable fituation, and DICK in the high road to happinefs, as he thought, when fortune, his *old friend*, contrived to defeat him in all his *promifed* joys. He never failed at a tavern amongft his affociates, to toaft his miftrefs in as many glaffes as fhe had letters in her name, a cuftom among the Romans formerly, and revived by the no lefs paffionate fighers of his days.

Nævia fex Cyathis, feptem Juftina bibatur.

BUT, O! ftrange reverfe, his mind was now occupied by mufing on the . . . . . .

———— Varium et mutabile femper
Fæmina ————————

and

and now and then he thought on Shakefpeare's,

" Frailty, thy name is *Woman*."

CHAGRINED and diffappointed, with quick feelings, and therefore irritable, DICK had re-courfe to his mafter-piece, the PEN; and being, as he fays himfelf, all *flame* and *fire*, no wonder that this *eclaircriffement* blazed fo violently over the county of Norfolk. The common *denoüe-ment* of this affair is too remote to our intention of *not* offending any of the parties living, or the memory of thofe deceafed, we fhall there-fore only premife, that in heat of paffion, and in refentment for (fuppofed) extreme ill ufage, it is well known he wrote

T H E

HISTORY of PUDICA,

A Lady of N — rf — lk.

With an Account of her Five Lovers;

Viz.

DICK MERRY-FELLOW,	JACK SHADWELL, of the
Count ANTIQUARY,	Lodge, and
Young 'Squire FOG, of	MILES DINGLEBOB, of
Dumpling-hall.	Popgun-hall, Efq.

Together

Together with

Miſs Pudica's Senſe of the Word Eclaircissement,

A N D A

Epithalamium on her Nuptials,

By *Tom Tenor*, Clerk of the Pariſh.

To the Tune of " Green grow the Ruſhes O'."

By William Honeycomb, Eſq.

Another and another ſtill ſucceeds,
And the laſt Fool's as welcome as the former.

                                            Rowe.

——————— *Ridiculum acri*
Fortius ac melius. ——————

                                            Hor.

London : Printed for M. Cooper, in Pater-Noſter Row.
M.DCC.LIV. *

---

* From the *Addenda* to the Monthly Review of February, 1754, we extraɛt the following article, and *critique*
upon it.

" The hiſtory of Pudica," &c. as above, " Oɛtavo. 1s.
" 6d. *Cooper.*—This appears to be the ſecret hiſtory of a
" young lady in real life, the incidents of which are put to-
" gether in a looſe and rambling manner ; but related with
" a good deal of pleaſantry, and ſome humour."

——————'Sdeath,

——— 'Sdeath, I'll print it,
And shame the fools.———

RESENTMENT, like that of Pope's poet, occa-
sioned the publication; which abounds with more
acrimonious humour, learning, and wit, than any
thing he has since wrote: and although it is not
our wish to revive the *fastidious story*, nor probe a-
fresh the feelings of those who received the wound
given by the venom'd shaft of malevolence, yet
we cannot, in justice to DICK's muse on that
occasion, omit the *Epithalamium.*

Welding-verses on the happy marriage of MILES
DINGLEBOB, *Esq. and* Madam his Lady, *by their
Honour's Pfalm singing Clerk,* Thomas Tenor, *of*
Popgun-hall, *in the County of* N—rf—lk.

Addressed to the Ringers of the Parish, *and to the
Tune of* " Green grow the Rushes O'."

I.

COME let us play at *jingle-bob,*
    Come let us play at *jingle-bob,*
    And I will sing,
    And you shall ring
For 'Squire and Madam DINGLEBOB.

II.

II.

Her four lovers may *go hoop*,
Her four, *&c.*
  The 'Squire o' the Hall
  Has flung them all,
By talking of the *chicken-coop*,

III.

I *Milly* take thee *Molly* O',
I *Milly*, *&c.*
  I am content,
  Nor do lament,
For all men have their *folly* O'.

IV.

JACK SHADWELL long'd to touch the gold,
JACK SHADWELL, *&c.*
  But trying to kifs
  The pretty Mifs,
PUDICA faid, *he was too old.*

V.

And young *'Squire* FOG began to *toy,*
And young, *&c.*
  O! no fays fhe,
  You're not for me,
No, *mafter*, I'll not have *a boy.*

VI.

Then *merry* DICK a letter fent,
'Then *merry*, *&c.*
  But O! the fun
  Was all undone,
By that d—n'd word *Eclairciffement.*

VII.

VII.

Then up arofe Count ANTIQUARY,
Then up, &c.
    What tho' they *fneer*
    At you, *my dear*,
You'll be a *Countefs*, Mrs. *Mary.*

VIII.

Suppofe that I don't like ye O',
Suppofe, &c.
    Sir *Count* enough,
    I'm for *better fluff*,
O! you don't know PUDICA O'.

IX.

The 'Squire I faw all *in his trim*,
The 'Squire, &c.
    And by the light
    'Twas fuch a *wight*,
I fcarcely could believe it him.

X.

And don't you think he was very wife?
And, &c.
    His eyes who faid,
    All in his head,
Appear'd like *two fcalt goofberries.*

XI.

Madam they fay was fond of *thapes*,
Madam, &c.
    And eke they fay,
    'Till t'other day,
In H—ll fhe dreaded *leading apes.*

XII.

XII.

Ring, my boys, O ! ring away,
Ring, my boys, &c.
    If right I think,
    We shan't want drink,
For 'tis the *Squire's wedding-day.*

XIII.

By and by the 'Squire to bed will go,
By and by, &c.
    Then we'll have done,
    Nor spoil the fun,
Until to-morrow's cock doth crow.

XIV.

If I aright again should think,
If I aright, &c.
    Why let me die,
    If by *her eye*,
I do believe she'll *sleep a wink.*

XV.

Green grow the rushes O',
Green grow, &c.
    No Duke so fine
    I do divine
Is happier with his Duchess O'.

" As when pale *Envy*, damning, crawls along,
" Guile in the heart, and gall beneath the tongue."

BAFFLED

BAFFLED in this his firſt love-projeᴄt, DICK,
in order to diſpel that ſplenetiᴄ melancholly natural to a *forſaken ſwain*, and to avoid imperti-
nent queſtions about the affair, *now become public*, retired to a friend's houſe, four miles from
Norwich, who was with DICK contemporaries at
Cambridge, but unfortunately for our hero, this
gentleman had *one fault*, if it can be ſo called,
he could not bear a pun, which made DICK, who
was often guilty of *punning*, more reſerved than
agreeable.

> *Pocentes vario multum diverſa palato.*
>
> HOR,

DICK ſeemed a little *below par* at dinner, *thinking*, we ſuppoſe, upon his late *amour*; but from
this he was ſoon relieved by the lively converſation of JACK FRIENDLY, a clergyman of great
wit and humour, and who underſtood *raillery* ſo
well, that DICK would, without any ſcruple,
apply to him what was ſaid of *Horace* by *Perſeus*.

> *Omne vafer vitium* ridenti FLACCUS *amico
> Tangit, & admiſſus* circum præcordia *ludit.*

DICK had recovered his uſual cheerfulneſs,

" Thou *Cheerfulneſs*, by Heav'n deſign'd
" To rule the pulſe that moves the mind,
" Whatever fretful paſſion ſprings,
" Whatever chance or nature brings,

" To

" To ftrain the tuneful poize within,
" And difarrange the fweet machine;
" Thou, goddefs, with a mafter-hand,
" Doft each attemper'd key command,
" Refine the foft, and fwell the ftrong,
" Till all is concord, all is fong."

and intirely forgot his miftrefs, when he received
advice of the death of a friend, and contemporary
at college, of whom he fays, " he was that ami-
" able character, fo feldom known in the world,
" *a man of whom all other men fpoke well.*"

Gratior & pulchra veniens in corpore virtus.

THE following epitaph DICK MERRY-FELLOW
wrote to his memory.

EDMUNDUS BACON BARONULUS,
Ævi Flos & Decus Sui
A. M. M.DCC.XLIII.
In Academia
Claruit.

A. M.DCC.XLIX.
Variolis correptus Occubuit.
Ætat. XXV.
Flevit SOROR, optima, pulcherrima,
De die in diem AMICI
Extinctum plorant,
Flet Soror, Flent Amici,
At Mater O ! ————————————

SEE!

See! mortal, where yon hallow'd tapers burn,
Another Bacon bearing to his urn;
Born with all charms, and bleft with ev'ry art
To win, to warm, to captivate the heart:
The joys of Virtue all the joys he knew,
Tho' brave, and fair, and gay, and young as you:
To footh affliction, or to foften pain,
He never fpoke, nor ever look'd in vain.
Love's fweeteft smiles fat blooming on his brow,
Graceful in all he did, as thou art now:
Love's fweeteft smiles, alas! too weak to fave,
See! doom'd, like thee, and victims to the grave:
Yet fhall he live, grim Tyrant, and defy,
Thy fting, O! Death, O! Grave, thy victory.
Far from the white-plum'd Hearfe Astrea fled,
The penfive Graces, weeping, hung the head;
Ev'n Envy figh'd, as fhe beheld the bier,
And from her eye burft forth th' unwilling tear.

O! friend, for let me call thee by that name,
What verse, O! fay, can give thee all thy fame?
Or to Britannia's fons his virtues tell,
Who died fo lovely, and who lived fo well!

Dick Merry-fellow having formerly learned
upon the flute abroad, was juft able *to fret a
pipe*, as Hamlet fays, though not to *play* upon
it; when requefted to entertain a company, he
was univerfally complimented on his *inclination
to oblige*, but feldom on his *play*, which, it muft
be confeffed, was not the moft harmonious: a
lady once told him, that rather than want *mufic*,
fhe would call in the firft *fow-gelder* with his
horn.

Mufic

Mufic has charms !

WE have already remarked, that DICK poffeffed
no fmall fhare of *vanity*, and fometimes confoled
himfelf in the pleafing idea of *having two firings
to his bow.* He took it into his head to imagine
that a lady, whom he calls CANIDIA, had a *liking*
for him ;

" Her *mind* was *virtue* by the *Graces* dreft."

and truly becaufe fhe approved herfelf the real
friend of PUDICA, by acquainting her with the
irregularities of our hero : " For, quoth he, it
" is no uncommon thing for a lady greatly and
" frequently to abufe the *object* of her *paffion*." As
a further proof of his confummate vanity, he
once told the father of PUDICA, " that it was not
he made love to his *daughter*, but his *daughter*
that made love to *him*."

What fhall I do? go hang myfelf? or marry?

MR. MERRY-FELLOW, during his temporary refidence in Norwich, preached in feveral of the
churches of that city, with popular applaufe :
one of his fermons is remembered, as being applicable to himfelf,—*On the Vanity of all human
Expectation.*

HE retired from the church foon after the
eclairciffement of the amour with PUDICA, being
only

only in Deacon's orders, and going abroad into
Germany, and afterwards into Ireland, he found
upon his return to England, in 1752, that *three*
gentlemen had, fince him, offered their *fervices*
to his *firft flame*, and that a young lady, who he
called Mifs BELL SHADWELL, was deceafed at
Bath.

" Not with lefs luftre Cleopatra fhin'd.
" The faireft, in her time, of woman-kind."

: To this lady our enterprizing hero had thought
proper to pay his addrefles before he went abroad;
and according to *his own* account, had kept up
a conftant correfpondence with her during his
ftay in Germany and Ireland, contrary to the
opinion of all her friends : but DICK thought
himfelf extremely ill ufed, that, as fhe had an independent fortune, fhe had neglected *to remember
him in her will.*

To trace the current upwards, as it flows,
And mark the fecret fpring, whence firft it rofe.

HER brother was the fourth admirer of PU-
DICA, and Mr. MERRY-FELLOW thought he had a
right to expect from him a catagorical account
of her illnefs and teftament, for which purpofe
he threatened him with a bill in Chancery, and
publicly affronted him at Thetford; but hearing that Mr. SHADWELL entertained a defign of
applying to the judges for a warrant to take him

up,

up, DICK fent the following letter in order to alleviate the bail, which was threatened to be laid at twenty thoufand pounds.

"To JOHN SHADWELL, Efq. at Buxton "Lodge, near Th—tf—d, N—rf—k.

"N——h, July, 1753.

"SIR,

"A report prevails at N——h, that you can-
"not, with fecurity to your own perfon, attend
"the fervice of your country at the enfuing
"affizes, as one of the Grand Jury, being un-
"der apprehenfions of *my taking you by the nofe,*
"or *caneing you,* or giving you the *difcipline of the*
"*horfewhip;* Sir, whatever treatment your un-
"generous conduct may deferve, *I honour the*
"*King's commiffion too much* to think of commit-
"ing a *violence* of any kind againft you; fo
"that I take this opportunity to declare, I have
"no intentions of molefting you in any fhape,
"and you may come to the *affizes* without meet-
"ing any interuption from,

"*Sir,*

"*Your humble Servant,*

"RICHARD MERRY-FELLOW."

D   THIS

THIS letter occafioned much converfation, and fome abufe, but DICK was a dangerous fellow to *meddle* with, and few dared to oppofe him *at his own weapons,* yet all thought him deferving the *rod.*

  " Obftructions made him eagerly afpire
  " All to furmount, and daring foar the higher."

WE are not able to trace our hero through the variety of extraneous incidents of his life, with that perfpicuity we could wifh, nor perhaps in juft chronology; nor do we mean to reflect on his memory by pointing out the pecuniary difficulties and odd adventures in which he at different periods was unfortunately involved. His wit and convivality rendered his company defirable by thofe fort of men *who live in a ftile,* and who were probably better able to fupport it than DICK, notwithftanding he had fo good a friend in the W-lp-le family; to whom, it has been fhrewdly faid, he bore fome *Relation.**

---

 * LOVE in a Tub, *an Eaftern Tale.*

 " ALGERNON, the fon of a rich and powerful *Vizier,*
 " fell defperately in love with a young and handfome vir-
 " gin, daughter of a perfon far beneath the rank and dig-
 " nity of fo great an heir apparent; his attachment was
        " favourably

In 1751, Dick Merry-fellow was abroad at
an univerfity in the Electorate of Hanover,
                                    - eftablifhed

" favourably accepted by the fair damfel, Drusilla, and
" mutual vows of fincere affection were exchanged. In
" this ftate of intrigue the happy pair continued fome
" time, till the difcovery made by fome officious friend to
" Seneca, put an end to the joys of *fecret* amour.

Times, ways, and means of meeting were deny'd;
But all thofe wants ingenious love fupply'd.

" In vain did Seneca infift on his fon's not thinking
" of Drusilla *in an honourable way*, but as often was
" he told, that no confideration of intereft nor filial
" duty fhould ever remove his regard for Drusilla into
" any other channel than that of Virtue, according to
" the hymeneal rites. Threats and promifes were inef-
" fectually tried to fhake this refolution : every expedient
" which craft or prudence could devife was oppofed to
" Algernon's paffion, but he ftill remained firm ; nor
" could the apprehenfion of being difinherited, alienate
" one fingle thought fayourable to his love !

Next, nay beyond his life ! he held her dear ;
She liv'd by him, and now he liv'd in her.

" Thus loving and beloved, Drusilla was fent into
" another part of the empire, and Algernon was pre-
" vailed on to fet out on his travels, with this provifo,
" that if he returned with the fame fentiments of inviol-
" able attachment to Drusilla, they fhould then be
" joined in the holy bans of matrimony, according to the
" cuftom of the country, for *Thelyphthora* was not yet
" publifhed

eſtabliſhed at Gottingen, by his late Majeſty
George II. and flouriſhing with an uncommon
number

" publiſhed. In this aſſurance, ALGERNON took his de-
" parture, though not without evident marks of reluct-
" ance; confidering himſelf as ſuffering an exile, arbi-
" trary, if not unjuſt.

" During a tour of three or four years into foreign
" countries, he ſigh'd many a tender wiſh towards the ill-
" fated DRUSILLA, and often, very often, committed the
" dictates of a chaſte paſſion to paper. Letters after
" letters were wrote, and ſent by him for DRUSILLA, but
" the politic SENECA had every letter which came to the
" general poſt-office, directed for her, opened and de-
" ſtroyed: In the ſame manner was every letter from her
" to ALGERNON detained. Thus deceived by appear-
" ances of neglect and infidelity, he preſſed ſeveral of his
" friends to inform him of DRUSILLA, but theſe letters
" were alſo intercepted. Various were his conjectures,
" all tending rather to embarraſs than quiet his mind—
" but he could not think DRUSILLA falſe!

" Detraction, that bane of happineſs! did not fail to
" be employed in conveying fuſpicions to the ears of our
" lovers:—ALGERNON was told that DRUSILLA was the
" coquette of faſhion, and DRUSILLA had accounts of
" ALGERNON's intrigues with grizettes and opera girls:—
" that he attended the toilet of the Pariſian beauties, and
" revelled in the brothels of Italy:—that his Seraglio at
" Conſtantinople exceeded the Grand Seignor's, and that
" he was the bon vivant of Spa: in ſhort, that he entered
" into all the follies and diſſipation which temptation,
" youth, and courts provoke.
" The

number of ſtudents for ſo early an inſtitution, and abounding with the moſt celebrated profeſ-
                                                            ſors

---

"" The watchful SENECA had provided for the iſſue of
" this manœuvere:—a reverend MUFTI, to whom SENECA
" had promiſed great preferments, was introduced to
" DRUSILLA as her future huſband, but, notwithſtand-
" ing that her love for ALGERNON was greatly abated,
" ſhe took refuge in an *apple-tree*, to avoid the importuni-
" ties of the MUFTI. This he might well have looked
" on as *ominous*, ſince the fruit of that fatal tree was eaten
" by the mother of ſin,

        Who for an apple damn'd mankind!

" However, after a few months practice of thoſe arts, by
" which the female heart is woo'd to compliance, the mar-
" riage of DRUSILLA and the MUFTI was celebrated, and
" SENECA hugged himſelf in the pleaſing idea of having
" prevented his ſon's contaminating the blood of the SENE-
" CA's with any thing below a hundred-thouſand pounder!
" but, alas! the vanity of all human expectations is found-
" ed in error, for, by fruſtrating a *legal* connection he cauſed,
" or brought on, an *adulterous* one.

        For all th' offence is in *opinion* plac'd,
        Which deems high birth by lowly choice debas'd.

" ALGERNON arrived from his travels, ignorant of the
" means and conſequences of the ſtratagem ſo ſucceſs-
" fully played off during his abſence, and was eaſily per-
" ſuaded to enter into an alliance with a lady of great
" fortune, but no ſooner was he made acquainted with
" the particulars of this unhappy affair, than he gave a

" looſe

fors in every fcience, one of whom, Dr. Albert
Haller, profeffor of phyfic, is known to all Europe,

" loofe to his feelings, and impuniffively enjoyed that fen-
" fual paffion he had fo long panted for, though in a
" manner lefs cenfurable.

" Where was the crime, if *pleafure* be procur'd
" Young, and a woman, and to blifs inur'd ?

DRYD.

" For many years this criminal *tetê-à-tetê* was carried
" on in the *face of day*. What every one knows no one
" is furprifed at ?—and the *cornuted* MUFTI pioufly wink-
" ed at that human frailty, which neither his authority nor
" admonition could redeem : nay, his duty, regard, and
" intereft, gave the lie to his feelings—as a hufband and
" paftor.

" Revenge is fweet! but never more fo than when it
" can be indulged with a juft fenfe of retaliation, and a
" gratification of libidinous defires.

What will not woman do, when need infpires
Their wit, or love their inclination fires !

" ALGERNON felt the force of this remark in the moft
" pointed manner, and the worthy MUFTI was the only
" one of the quartetto who bore the antlers with ftoical
" fortitude."

☞ Our only motive for introducing the above Tale,
along with the Memoirs of DICK MERRY-FELLOW, is,
that the account DICK MERRY-FELLOW often gave of
his own life and actions, refembled fo ftrongly thofe of a
fon of the wife of the MUFTI, that he was wont to fay,
and with fome degree of exultation, " that he believed
" HE had NOBLE *blood in his veins*."

rope, and held in high efteem in the learned world.
There were many *Engliſh* at this time finiſhing their
ſtudies there, particularly the Marquis of Cær-
narvon, now Duke of Chandos, a young nobleman of very extraordinary merit, and was looked
upon as an honour to his country, and the Engliſh nobility in general; being a man of un-
tainted morals, and the moſt regular conduct;
addicted to no vices, and purſuing his ſtudies
with an application unuſual to men of his age
and rank; of an obliging carriage; with all the
dignity, but without the pride of quality; of
great evennefs of temper, which nothing was
obſerved to warm ſo much, as his attachment to
his friends, and countrymen; and ſo engaging
even to a ſtranger on his firſt appearance, that
it was impoffible to be in his company, and not
recollect immediately of what family he was by
that diſtinguiſhing characteriſtic;

" Thus gracious CHANDOS is beloved at ſight."

POPE.

AT the ſame time with his Grace, were Mr.
Stanhope, Captain Robertſon of the Royal Iriſh,
the Honble. Mr. Hobart, ſon of the late Earl of
Buckinghamſhire, all of them extremely careſſed,
and in great efteem with the ſeveral profeſſors;
the latter of whom attained to a perfection of

ſpeaking

fpeaking *High-Dutch*, with an accuracy fcarcely inferior to a German, converfing much with the ftudents of the country, to whom he was very agreeable, having all the politenefs and addrefs of his father.

HAPPY in the company and acquaintance, *dulce fodalitium*, of fuch friends as thefe, Mr. MERRY-FELLOW was feldom known *to heave the figh of difappointed love*, to be *abfent* in converfation, or to have the *mind's eye* for ever turned upon the beauties of the *enchanted* caftle, and ruminating upon the charms of his *imprifoned Dulcinea*; he was not

L'Homme qui ne fe trouve point & ne fe trouvera jamais.

Other joys fat lighter on his breaft, and were the companions of his heart, till the departure of his friends, who, fome months after his arrival, fet out for Blois and Orleans in France, leaving the profeffors, as well as their countrymen, in great regret upon that occafion.

Mr. MERRY-FELLOW ftaid not for any long continuance after them, but before he went away, was complimented by the Pro-rector, an officer much in the nature of our Vice-chancellor, with an offer of the degree of *Doctor of Laws*; their public time of conferring their degrees, and which

which anſwers to our commencement or act, fall-
ing out before he left the Univerſity: this he
declined as thinking it too great an honour for
one in his ſtation of life, and after expreſſing
the warmeſt ſenſe he could of that mark of eſteem
in the Pro-rector, begged leave to be excuſed
from accepting it. The Pro-rector obligingly
refuſed to take his anſwer then, and defired him
to confider of it till next day, when he returned
back to him in the ſame ſentiments.

" *Let* Pallas *dwell in towers herſelf has rais'd.*"

FROM Gottingen he went to Hanover to join
the late Honble. Captain Robert Boyle Walfingham, who was then on his return to England, with whom, and Count Sch-l-nb-rg, a
nobleman of great abilities, and eſteemed one of
the beſt officers in the King's ſervice, he ſpent
many agreeable hours in the delightful gardens
of Herenhauſen, admiring the beauties of art
and nature, diſperſed in ſuch profuſion in every
part of them, and particularly the *Jet-d'Eau* in
the center, ſo juſtly eſteemed the fineſt in Europe,
and perhaps it is unrivalled in the whole world.
It rifes on ordinary occaſions to a perpendicular
height of eighty feet, and when his Majeſty is
refiding at the palace, to one hundred and twenty.

COUNT Sch-l-nb-rg was maſter of a great
deal of wit and humour, which rendered his converſation

verfation extremely lively and entertaining, and always accompanied his defcriptions, which on that account never failed to divert as well as inftruĉt; to the pleafures of whofe acquaintance, and that of ⸱his friend Captain Walfingham, we doubt not Mr. MERRY-FELLOW dedicated much of his time.

H E returned to England in Oĉtober, where he ftayed but a few days till he fet off for Ireland, whether he went⸱with Captain Walfingham,* Aid-de-Camp to the Duke of Dorfet, and fon of the Speaker of the Houfe of Commons in that kingdom, fince created Earl of Shannon, and by whom he was received with all that politenefs for ages remarkable in the Boyle family; but that great man did not confine his favours to himfelf only; he introduced him to the acquaintance of the firft people of fafhion in Ireland, by which means he had the moft advantageous opportunies of informing himfelf of the conflitution and intereft of that kingdom; and as the Speaker's houfe was ever open to him, of improving what little knowledge he had, and

---

* This worthy, but unfortunate friend of DICK's, was lately caft away in the Thunderer, a feventy four, of which he was Captain.

> Non ille pro caris amicis
> Aut patria timidus perire.
> HOR.

the

the frequent obfervations he made by the converfation of men of rank and learning; and what
was the moft of all regarded by him, the daily
fatisfaction of being admitted into the prefence
and company of that illuftrious PATRIOT, and to
admire his unwearied diligence for the fervice
and good of his country, and his unalterable
fteadinefs in the purfuit of it;—virtues that muft
tranfmit his memory to the laft rolls and records
of eternity.

" ———— Man, each man's born
" For the high bufinefs of the public good."

WITH this great example for ever before their
eyes, it is no wonder to fee the Commons of that
kingdom fired with a zeal for liberty and honour,
and rifing to a pitch of ROMAN virtue; it is
emulation working ftrongly in a noble mind, that
parent and fource of all true greatnefs, and brings
conviction to this *fidling* age; what infinite importance it is poffible for one fhining character to
be of to a whole nation, even in thofe for-ever-to-
be-dreaded times, in all ftates of freedom, when
public fpirit fleeps, when nodding juftice repofes
in the chair of indolence, and nothing throughout the land is broad awake,—but private intereft
and general corruption.

DURING Mr. MERRY-FELLOW's ftay in Ireland,
he was prefent at many debates in the Honourable

able Houfe of Commons, and had frequent op-
portunities of admiring the ferenity and wifdom
of the Speaker, the great abilities of the Prime
Serjeant, Mr. M--l--ne, the clearnefs and perfpicuity of the Mafter of the Rolls, the eloquence of Sir Richard Cox, the dignity of Sir
Alexander Gore, the honefty of heart in Mr.
Charles Gardiner, the rifing virtues of Colonel
Richard Boyle, and the eagernefs and warmth
of Colonel Difkes.

PLACEMEN and penfioners forgot all *private*
views, and anfwered the call of liberty and of
truth ! and officers gave the unbiaffed vote, warm
as is their nature in the caufe of freedom;
amongft thefe latter will be remembered the
names of N--pp--r and Walfingham.

In the Houfe of Peers it was impoffible to
enter without remarking the never-to-be-equalled
integrity of the Earl of Kildare, the folidity
and judgment of the Earl of Carrick, the learning of the Bifhop of Derry. In a word, Mr.
MERRY-FELLOW has been often heard to fay,
there were fo many characters in that kingdom,
eminently diftinguifhed for all inftances of *public fpirit* and *national honour*, that it was to be
recommended to a young noblemen, entering on
his travels, not by any means to put an end
to them, till he had paid a vifit on that fide of
the

the water; it is true he might acquire addrefs
and flattery in *France*, mufic and virtù in *Italy*,
honour and gravity in *Spain*, commercial arts in
Holland; in *Germany*, he might learn ferenity
and courage; but to be a TRUE PATRIOT, he
muft go to *Ireland*.

> " I own the glorious fubject fires my breaft,
> " And my foul's darling paffion ftands confeft."
>
> ROWE.

WHILE Mr. MERRY-FELLOW was preparing to
leave Ireland, he received a letter, informing
him of the death of Mifs BELL SHADWELL, of
the fmall-pox at Bath; the fhock was fo great,
having had, as he fays, a letter from her in
good health, * but a few days before, and dated
within ten days of her deceafe, that it threw
him into a fever. He recovered from this diforder, went into deep mourning for her, and
fought variety of company in order to divert his
mind from thinking of her; but ftill there appeared in his countenance, on all occafions, a
vifible diftraction of foul.

> Anfwer, my foul! whence this unmanly woe?
> Speak, eyes! why ftarts th' involuntary tear?

HE returned to England in July, 1752, when
arriving at London, he fell ill of the fmall-pox, at

---

* In another part of DICK's narrative, he fays, " fhe lan-
" guifhed two months."

the

the age of twenty-nine, and although extremely
dangerous, he purfued his journey down to Thetford in great pain; from whence he went next day
to Norwich, travelling in the greateſt agony of
mind and body, where, being put under the care
of one of the ableſt phyſicians in the world, the late
Doƈtor Offley, and who, with the greateſt knowledge in his profeſſion, was certainly one of the
beſt men that lived, he ſoon recovered. The
marks of the diſorder, which he carried to his
grave, was certainly a mortifying circumſtance
to a man of gallantry and intrigue, and who at
all times thought himſelf rather *handſome* than
otherwiſe. Beauty, according to Shakeſpeare, is

> A fleeting good, a gloſs, a glaſs, a flow'r,
> Loſt, faded, broken, dead—within an hour.

WE have, in ſome degree, anticipated the violent meaſures purſued by DICK to oblige Mr.
SHADWELL to produce the will of his deceaſed
ſiſter, and are not at all ſorry that we have got
over that moſt diſagreeable part of his memoir :
it will be neceſſary, however, juſt to mention,
that the incomparable PUDICA, heireſs to between forty and fifty thouſand pounds, was to be
married to her *fifth* lover MILES DINGLEBOB,
Eſq. who, it is ſaid, had twenty-ſix thouſand
pounds left him by an uncle:

——— *Quod*

——— *Quod optanti divûm promittere nemo*
Auderet, volvenda dies en! attulit ultrò.

.THE nuptials over, and the lady in poſſeſſion
of a huſband, in whom the perfections of her firſt
four admirers are centered, viz.

> The *humour* of DICK MERRY-FELLOW,
> The *learning* of COUNT ANTIQUARY,
> The *beauty* of young 'SQUIRE FOG,
> And the *bravery* of JACK SHADWELL.

DICK, who never miſſed an opportunity of
playing off his artillery of wit, complimented
the hymeneal rites with a poetical *feu de joye*, by
way of Epithalamium, or wedding-ſong; * and
ſoon after produced his hiſtory of PUDICA;
written, as we have been told, within the pre-
cincts of the Fleet-priſon, and publiſhed in
1754.

THE ſeverity and pointed ridicule with which
every circumſtance of that affair is told, ſhews
him to have been a man of the boldeſt conceits,
which he never checked nor modified by reaſon,
but went on from one extreme to another, till
the *public*, to whom he always appealed, and endeavoured to draw in as partiſans with *his* diſ-
putes, became ſatiate, and wearied of his perpetual clack.

* See Page 24, &c.

Short

Short of it's aim, and impotent to wound,
The feeble shaft falls hurtlefs to the ground.

YET DICK perfevered, and feemed to triumph o'er the filence of the adverfe parties, who held in ineffable contempt the author who eftablifhes his own fuccefs, on that felf-approbation which is derived from vanity alone, as Horace expreffes it,

Gaudent fcribentes, et fe venerantur.

From felf each fcribbler adoration draws,
And gathers incenfe from his own applaufe.

WHAT efpecially gives difguft to ill-natured writings, is, that they convey an idea of the author's felf-fufficiency, and fuppofed fuperiority, which few are willing to confefs without retalliation. Hence it is, that we perceive general fatirifts are univerfally detefted and defpifed, as vermin who breed in the wounds of fociety, or hypocrites, who infinuate their own purity, by afperfing and defiling the reft of mankind.

'Tis an old maxim in the fchools,
That vanity's the food of fools;
Yet now and then your men of wit
Will condefcend to take a bit.

SWIFT.

THE rapid fale of a publication will fometimes induce the author to believe every purchafer

chafer becomes a deponent in favour of his caufe, or an admirer of his virtues and, learning, when in fact the avidity with which people read ludicrous works, whether in profe or of metrical compofition, only arifes, as Puff fays in the Critic—*becaufe they ought not to read them.*

" And each fworn fool, I fwear, has his fworn brother."

THESE remarks, though prematurely given, may ferve as the criterion of moft of our heroe's *hafty* productions—but not of his *ferious* ones.

THE R-y-l Regifter, Nocturnal Revels, the Bevy of Beauties, Sketches from Nature, the Abbey of Kilkhampton, the Diabo-lady, Modern Characters from Shakefpeare, and from the Beggar's Opera; the Tête à Tête, the Cabinet, the Hackney Coach, and fuch-like ftrictures on the conduct and foibles of individuals, are more acceptable to the bulk of common readers than the works of Gibbon, Hume, Robertfon, Moore, Dalrymple, Wraxhall, Burney, Beattie, and the many other learned and ingenious authors of our time. One would imagine from the univerfal tafte for detraction and malevolent cenfure, that we were all bred up in the " School for Scandal."

But, train'd to ill, and harden'd in its crimes,
The pen, relentlefs, kills through future times.

O_F

OF the many effays, political and fatirical,. which the prefs, and bookfeller's fhelves now groan under, few of them are directed by any other motive than party-fpirit, or affaffination of character, and, excepting *Anticipation* by the lively pen of Mr. T—l, and the *Abbey of Kilk-hampton* by Mr. F—, none of them have lite- rary merit; yet thefe wafps of folly and diffipa- pation, fancy themfelves borne, like blazing ftars among the clouds, to the admiration of the gaz- ing multitude :

And up he rifes like a vapour,
Supported high on wings of paper;
He finging flies, and flying fings,
While from below all *Grub-ftreet* rings.

SWIFT.

BUT, to have done with the *London* dealers in fcandal, we muft return to the narrative of DICK MERRY-FELLOW, who, we pronounce, was as happy at the knack of writing lampoons, ad- vertifements extraordinary, fneers, hand-bills, far- cafms, allarms, fongs, fquibs, and electioneering rattles, as any of the fhort-lived heroes of attic abode,

" Who deal out libels—wholefale and retail."

The

The following S O N G,

Wrote by DICK MERRY-FELLOW about the
year 1754, is the moſt perfeᵭt copy of it we
are able to procure.

TO you, fair LADIES of the field!
  Wᴇ SPORTSMEN now indite;
To you our morning pleaſures yield,
  And think of you at night:
Tho' *hares* and *foxes* run a-pace,
'Tis beauty gives the fineſt *chace.*

II.

The morning roſe, and with a fog,
  Incloſ'd the heath all round;
So thick we ſcarce could ſee a *dog,*
  Ten yards upon the ground:
Yet we to ELDEN took our way,
True SPORTSMEN never mind the day.

III.

Like VENUS (if ſhe was ſo fair
  As antient poets feign,
With coral lip and golden hair,
  Juſt riſing from the main)
We ſaw the lovely BELL appear,
Nor miſs'd the fun when ſhe was near.

IV.

At ELDEN, on a trail we hit,
  And ſoon the *hare* we found,

Whᴇn

When up fhe ftarted from a pit,
    And ftretch'd along the ground :
Hark forward ! all the SPORTSMEN cry'd,
Hark forward ! hills and dales reply'd.

V.

Quite crofs the country, and away
    She fled in open view ;
Our HUNTSMAN was the firft to fay,
    " She ran not but fhe flew :"
Whilft BILLY GRIGSON rode and fwore,
" 'Twas old MOTHER ROGERS gone before."

VI.

With pleafure GREENE the *chace* purfu'd,
    Nor wifh'd for mufic then ;
But often as the *hare* he view'd,
    In raptures he began :—
" Tell me, ye gods ! if any founds
" Be half fo fweet as t' hear the hounds."

VII.

Thus for an hour, all in full cry,
    We nimbly tript along ;
Nor thought that MADAM was to *die*,
    Nor we to have a SONG :
Says SLAPP, " though now fhe runs fo faft,
" Brave boys ! we'll put her down at laft."

VIII.

Kind fate indulg'd an hour more,
    And back fhe turn'd again ;
Such fport fure ne'er was feen before,
    But all her turns were vain :

For

For *Butler*, foremoſt of the *pack*,
And *Frolick* ſeiz'd her by the back.

IX.

To THETFORD then, our ſport being done,
In ſpirits we repair;
Where GARDINER a ſong began,
In honour of] the fair:
And as the merry chorus riſe,
We all to Shadwell turn'd our eyes.

THIS juvenile foŋg, though deſcriptive of a chaee, in which DICK was not only in purſuit of *pleaſure* but of *profit*, is, by no means, a poetical compoſition of merit, either in harmony of numbers, or aptitude of fancy: its being local rendered it. a favourite air at the time it was wrote, but it is now little known, and leſs admired, when put in competition with his latter productions.

FROM the year 1754 to the 27th of March 1757, we are at a loſs to ſay, preciſely, what was our heroe's purſuit, but ſuppoſe it in the ſervice of his country, a line of life he ſeemed moſt attached to, and every way qualified for; and though we may not have an opportunity of recording him as a Marleborough, a Eugene, a Saxe, a Berwick, a Granby, a Pruſſia, a Wolfe, or a Waſhington, whither in reſpect to
E 3   diſcipline,

difcipline or general tactic, or, in what is more valuable than either—success.

——— *Militavi non fine gloria.*

H o R.

Yet we muft allow him the merit of *meaning well,* which is as much as is ufually faid now a-days, of any officer who is not as *intrepid* as a Tarleton, as *indefatigable* as a Cornwallis, as *determined* as a Prevoft, as *cool* as a Wafhington, as *bold* as a Wallace, as *modeft* as a Parker, as *brave* as a Pearfon, and as *lucky* as a Rodney :—to be *rich* and *politic* are ftubborn arguments in favor of a great officer !

THIS three years of lapfe in our memoir, is a *hiatus,* according to Doctor Bently's expreffion in his criticifms, *non valdè deflendus :* however, this paufe, if we may fo call it, fhall not be filled up *by us* with immaginary occurrences, as is frequently the cafe in hiftory of guefs-work, which is delivered down to pofterity little better than

" A tale told by an ideot."

SHAKESPEARE.

ON the 27th of March, 1757, DICK MERRY-FELLOW was promoted from being Lieutenant of Granadiers in the 12th regiment of foot, to a com-a company of marines. This 12th regiment was the famous patriotic regiment which, when commanded by James II. either to lay down their arms, or to use them in support of measures unconftitutional, arbitrary, and contrary to the religion, the laws, and liberties of this Kingdom; to the great difappointment and confufion of the King, all to a man laid down their arms!

" Rome boafts her fons, a race of ftubborn fools,
" To virtue train'd by grey-beard Cato's rules:"

HERE we have another *hiatus valdè deflendus*, till the ever-glorious year 1759—an æra of Britifh hiftory which will be admired as long as the annals of this Country can be read!

And fure that tale for Britons muft have charms,
That fhews you France fubdu'd by Britifh arms:

IN this ever-memorable year, our hero commanded a detachment of marines on board the *Rippon* man of war of 60 guns, Captain Edward Jekyll, at the fiege of *Guadelupe*, when that fhip was oppofed to two ftrong Batteries of the French in the capital town of *Baffe-Terre*, was on fhore during the whole of the engagement, which lafted ten hours, and once on fire: the fhip in that action fired 1300 great fhot, and the marines 2000 cartridges; fo great was the ardor

E 4

of

of the men, that when all' the grape-fhot on
board, and wadding for the canon was expended, the feamen and marines made wadding
of their fhirts and jackets, and fired them
away at the trenches of the enemy.

THE *Rippon* was alfo engaged, but a few days
before, at *St. Pierre's*, the capital of Martinico, or
Martinique, againft four batteries of canon and a
bomb-battery, which continued throwing fhells
for four hours, few of which fell at a greater
diftance than thirty or forty yards from the
fhip: many of them burft in the fea along-fide
of the *Rippon*, which appeared like boiling water, and one in particular fell between the barge
and yawl.

O F this expedition to the Weft-Indies, againft
Martinico and Guadelupe, and other the Leeward
Iflands, fubjeft to the French King, CAPTAIN
MERRY-FELLOW wrote a very clear and circum-
ftantial account,

Verfas ad Littora Puppes
Refpiciunt, totumque allabi claffibus Æquor.

VIRG.

Imperi
Porreƈa Majeflas, ab Ortu
Solis ad Hefperium Cubile
Cuflode Rerum C Æ S A R E.——

. H OR.

a *third*

a *third edition* of which, in quarto, Englifh and French, was publifhed in 1762.

THE dedication to the Queen, is dated at Lincoln, where he then refided, February 6, and is a modeft and elegant compofition; on prefenting of which he had the honor to kifs her Majefty's hand, being introduced by the late Earl Delawar.

THIS journal commences about the latter end of October, 1758, when Captain Hughes in the Norfolk, with a fquadron of men of war and a fleet of tranfports, fail'd from Spithead, and, owing to contrary winds, did not join the fhips and tranfports from Plymouth Sound till November 15, lat. 49° 40', when the whole fquadron confifted of the following men of war and bomb veffels, with 60 fail of tranfports.

Norfolk   74   St. George 90   Berwick   64
Panther   60   Burford -   70   *Rippon* - 60
Lyon -   60   Winchefter 50   Renown   30
                 Bomb Veffels.
Infernal, Granada, King's Fifher, Falcon.

IN the tranfports were the following regiments, with a detachment of the artillery from Woolwich, Old Buffs, Duroure's, Elliot's, Barrington's, Watfon's, Armiger's

ON

ON board the feveral men of war, the marines were augmented to the number of 800, and were intended to be formed into a battalion, under the command of a Lieutenant-Colonel and Major, in order to land with the troops, and do duty in the line, but this difpofition was expreflly difappro- ved by Commodore Moore at Barbadoes, who refufed to land the marines.

THE general officers employed on this expedi- tion were Major-general Hopfon, commander in chief; Major-general Barrington, Colonels Armiger and Haldane, and Lieutenant Colonels Trapaud and Clavering, as Brigadiers.

AFTER a paffage of feven weeks and three days, without any very material occurrences intervening, the armament appeared off the Ifland of Barba- does on Wednefday, January 3, 1759, and came to anchor in Carlifle Bay, N. lat. 13° 5', long. W. 59°.

IN this, our epitome of DICK's expedition to the Weft-Indies, we do not mean to trouble the reader with nautical obfervations, natural hif- tory, and the dull rotine of defcription by navi- gators, but fimply to follow our hero in chronolo- gical order.

AT

AT Barbadoes the fquadron received a reinforcement of 200 Highlanders belonging to the
fecond battalion of Ld. John Murray's regiment,
and forty Negroes, on board each line-of-battle-
fhip. With this force, confiderably impaired by
ficknefs, not exceeding 5000 effective men, the
Commodore and General fet fail from Carlifle Bay
on Saturday, January 13, and ftood for the Ifland
of Martinico, diftant about forty leagues, which
they made next morning, N. lat. 14° 30', long.
W. 61°,

The whole fleet entered the Bay of Port-Royal
on the 15th, and the marines from the *Rippon* and
Briftol land. Next day the firft attack was made,
and Fort-Negro carried, in which DICK had a
fprig of the laurel ! As the fquadron approached
Port-Royal, the garrifon of the citadel began to
throw large fhells from mortars, at two miles and
1174 yards fall; and the troops were landed
without oppofition, but on the day following
were re-embarked.

VARIOUS have been the reafons affigned for
this very precipitate retreat from Martinico,—for
it fince appears that the enemy were not in force,
and that we had only one officer and 22 men
killed, and two officers and 47 men wounded, in
the attempt.

JANUARY

JANUARY 18th, the fquadron weighed, and next morning made into the fpacious bay of *St. Pierre,* with a wefterly wind, a circumftance fo very uncommon in this latitude, that the enemy here, and afterwards at Guadelupe, on the Englifh fleet having the fame advantage of wind, declared, " it was a judgment from heaven, and that the " Englifh were fent to punifh them for their fins." Somewhat like what is reported to have been faid by a Britifh officer formerly, at the fiege of Calais, who being afked by an infolent Frenchman, on the furrender of the town to the Duc de Guife, " when he intended to crofs the fea back, " and take poffeffion of it again ;" replied, " when your fins are greater than ours."

" *Nous y rentrerons, quand vos pèches feront plus*
" *Grandes que les notres.*"

O! nimium Dilecte Deo! cui Militat Æther
Et conjurati veniunt ad Claffica venti.

CLAUDIEN.

THIS thought is beautifully exemplified in Mr. ADDISON's fimile of the *Deftroying Angel,* applied to the Duke of Marleborough, in the celebrated poem of the CAMPAIGN.

As when an angel, by divine command,
With rifing tempefts fhakes a guilty land ;
(Such as of late o'er pale *Britannia* paft)
Calm and ferene he drives the furious blaft :

Calm

And pleas'd th' Almighty's orders to perform,
Rides in the whirlwind, and directs the storm.

THESE elegant lines DICK endeavoured to render into *Latin* tho' infinitely below the original.

Sic Raphael divinâ ferens Mandata per Auras,
Impia cum Quatiat furgentibus Arva procellis,
(Qualis in Angliacas nupèr defœviit Oras)
Subridens mediâ nimborum in Noêti corufcat,
Lœtitiâ exultans ; Divoque jubente, tremendo
Turbine fertur Eques, cohibetque furentis Habenas.

R. G.

The *Rippon* being ordered to filence a battery
one mile and a half north of the town, about
two o'clock let go her anchor within half a cable's
length of the fhore, in thirty-five fathom water,
and engaged the Fort and fmaller batteries for
four hours and a half pretty *warmly*. During
this action, DICK MERRY-FELLOW offered to land
with the marines under his command, but was
refufed permiffion by Captain Jekyll ; the confequence of which had liked to have proved fatal
to the fhip, as the enemy returned to their guns
and rack'd her fore and aft, in fo much, that it
was thought advifable to cut her cable and return to the fleet.

In

In the morning of the 20th, the Commodore made fail, and next day was joined off Dominica by the Amazon and two tranfports from Antigua, with 200 men of Colonel Rofs's regiment; as did alfo the Spy floop, N. lat. 15°, long. W. 60°. On the 22d, the fquadron appeared off the Ifland of *Guadelupe*, N. lat. 16°, long. W. 61°, and in the evening, the plan of attack on the citadel and batteries of *Baffe-Terre*, was given out in orders by the commander in chief, to commence upon a fignal next morning.

At half paft feven, on the 23d, the men of war ran down clofe along fhore, and at nine the general attack was made by all the fhips, with great fpirit, judgment and fuccefs. The *Rippon* engaged the *Morne-Rouge*, a battery of fix guns, but having run in too clofe, on letting her anchor go, fhe tailed the fhore and ftuck faft. Thus expofed to the fire of *Le Morne-Rouge*, and a feven-gun battery on her ftarboard-bow, fhe cut the cable and hawfer, and continued engaged with great difadvantage, till reinforced by the Briftol of fifty guns.

At three o'clock, the militia of the ifland brought up an eighteen pounder, which played upon the *Rippon,* in the way of *batterie en barbe,* for two hours. Many of the men being killed or wounded, the fhip on fire, occafioned by a large

large box, containing 900 cartridges, having blown up, and the grape-fhot and wadding being expended, the *Rippon* was obliged to fling out a fignal of diftrefs, when the Briftol came to her relief, and at twelve at night fhe hove off.

At ten o'Clock, the town of *Baffe-Terre* blazed one general conflagration, by the fhells and car-cafes thrown from the four bomb-veffels which were ordered clofe in fhore as foon as the batteries had been filenced, and continued to play upon the town and citadel all night. During the en-gagement of this day, the fquadron fuftained but little lofs of men. The *Rippon*, upon the whole, fuffered as much as any fhip.

Next day, the Commodore anchored in the road, and in the afternoon the troops were landed and found the town and citadel abandoned, which they took immediate poffeffion of. We were, now joined by the Buckingham of fixty-four guns, and other fhips from Barbadoes.

January 25, the enemy appeared to the num-ber of 2000, throwing up intrenchments with a defign to defend the Governor's head-quarters, and the *Dos d'Ane*, to the laft extremity. A flag of truce was fent the day following to *Le Cheva-lier Nadau Dutriel*, the Governor, offering him terms, which he refufed in a very fpirited an-fwer,

fwer, and had it fucceeded to a gallant defence of *Baffe-Terre*, could not have failed of doing him honour. Had he been really brave, he fhould have acted like another *Turnus*,

> *Rapit acer,*
> *Totam aciem in teucros, et contrâ in littore fiftit.—*
> *Ultro occurramus ad undam,*
> *Dum trepidi, egreffifque labant vefligia prima.*
> Æn. 10.

THIS was the time to have difplayed undaunted refolution and obftinacy of defence; for if it was true, that the poffeffion of the metropolis became fo eafy an acquifition to the invaders, to whom was it owing, that it was not made more difficult? menaces of refiftance *jufqu' à l'Extremitè* are noble, but it is then only when they are thrown out fword in hand, the bayonet pointed, and not the pen; the fhore difputed inch by inch, and the approaching enemy defied in arms at the water's edge, not by letters at a diftance. His epiftle was therefore confidered by the Englifh officers, as the fanfaronade of a man who had not a heart to execute, if a head to defign, and in whom timidity would render abortive, whatever under-ftanding might infpire.

IN confequence of this refufal to come into terms of capitulation, the inhabitants of *Baffe-Terre* fuffered great hardfhips, and the troops burnt the

canes

canes and fcoured the country for many days, during which time frequent fkirmifhing enfued.

FEBRUARY 6, a ftrong naval force, with two bombs and three tenders, with a large detachment of marines from the other fhips, failed to the eaftward for *Grande-Terre*, and on the 10th the Panther was fent as a reinforcement. On the 13th, Fort Louis, at *Grande-Terre*, was taken after a fevere cannonading for fix hours, and the enemy drove from their entrenchments by the marines and Highlanders with fixed bayonets.

FEBRUARY 14, the *Rippon* and Spy failed this morning, with 500 fick and wounded from the regimental hofpital on board of eight tranfports, for St. John's Town, Antigua, North lat. 17°. long. W. 61°. 20′. The *Rippon* having performed this fervice, returned and anchored in *Baffe-Terre* Road, on the 22d, where DICK found affairs much in the fame pofture he had left them eight days before.

THE French, on the ifland, tried every ftratagem they could devife to draw our men out into the fun, whofe meridian rays they well knew were fatally powerful on European conftitutions, and by thefe artifices they vainly flattered themfelves to weary out the Englifh troops: we had

F   indeed

indeed 1800 men of the army fick or dead at this time.

Major General Hopfon died at head-quarters on the 27th, when the command devolved on Major General Barrington. The fame evening ˙the Rippon and Briſtol were ordered to cruize off the iſland of St. Euſtatia, to prevent *our good friends* the Dutch, from fupplying the enemy with proviſions, &c. which they had conſtantly done from the time the Engliſh took poſſeſſion of *Baſſe-Terre.*

Early in March, the batteries were blown up and deſtroyed, the whole army embarked on board the tranſports, leaving the Engliſh Go-vernor and a garriſon in the citadel, and a naval force to cover it; the Commodore with the fleet failed for *Grande-Terre,* where they anchored on the 11th, and found the marines in poſſeſſion, but very fickly. On the 13th, our ſquadron failed for Prince Rupert's Bay, Do-minica, diſtant nine leagues, in conſequence of hearing that eight fail of the line and three frigates, under *Monſieur* Du Bompar, was then at Port-Royal. This retrogade motion of ours was of infinite advantage to the enemy's priva-teers, who took not leſs than between eighty and ninety fail of Engliſh merchantmen, which they carried into Martinico, after the cruizers (the

Rippon and Briftol) were called in, in eleven weeks.

'But, to pafs over all thefe after-thoughts, we fhall briefly add, that affairs wore a gloomy afpeét at *Baffe-Terre*, where the French often en-. gaged the attention of the garrifon, and our Go- vernor, Lieut. Colonel Defbrifay, * and Major Trollop, were both blown up by a powder ma- gazine, while they were reconnoitering the enemy with a telefcope.

The Englifh after this, feemed to gain fome par- tial advantage here at and *Grande-Terre*, by fallies from the garrifon, but we afterwards failed in an attempt on the Guadelupe fide of the ifland.

April

---

* This gallant commander was a Captain of foot at the battle of *Rocoux*, near *Liege*, in 1746; where being wounded, and lying upon the ground amongft the flain, he was run through by a French officer, whofe unmanly example was immediatly followed by the platoon he com- manded; all, or moft of them planting their bayonets in different parts of his body: of about thirteen wounds which he received, eight were judged to be mortal : being afterwards at table with the *Marechal* Count de Saxe, of whofe politenefs as an enemy, many honourable inftances were given in the courfe of that war, he was ftrongly fo- licited by the *Marechal* to tell him " who the officer was " that ufed him fo unlike a foldier, threatening to dif-

F 2   " grace

April 12, a detachment of 1300 men, under Brigadier Clavering, &c. landed and carried a ftrong entrenchment, with the lofs of one officer and nineteen men killed, and two officers and thirty-two men wounded : this advantage was fo effectually improved, that with the affiftance of Captain Uvedale of the Granada bomb, he took the fort at *Petit-Bourg,* of *Mahant,* of *Guoyave,* of St. *Mary's,* &c.

AT this time, April 19, the bravery of our troops had got the better of every obftacle, had forced the enemy in all their entrenchments and ftrong paffes, had taken fifty pieces of canon, and had advanced as far as the *Capefterre,* the only remaining unreduced part of the country. This at laft brought the French to terms and articles of capitulation, which were figned on Tuefday, May 1, 1759.

" grace him at the head of the regiment;" but *Defbrifay,* though well acquainted with the name, the commiffion he bore, and the corps he ferved in, moft generoufly declined it ; contented with letting his Excellency know, that he was not a ftranger to his perfon, and begging his excufe from being obliged to point him out. So magnanimous an inftance of Britifh worth, deferves to be recorded to pofterity ! as it reflects honor on the memory of a good chriftian and foldier.

Monfieur

Monsieur Du Bompar, with a force from Martinico, landed in another part of the ifland, but
hearing of its furrender, re-embarked his men
and retreated to Port-Royal, whilft the Englifh
fleet lay inactive in Prince Rupert's Bay, Dominica.
DICK MERRY-FELLOW very freely cenfures the
conduct of Commodore Moore, in not *looking fharp*
to the motions of the French fleet. "Certain it is,
" that if he had *kept an eye* upon them, (not to be
" fufpected of a pun upon this occafion) it was
" not an HAWK's eye."

MAY 2, our fleet left Dominica, and next day
were off the ifland of Marigalante, in lat. 16°. N.
For four days we were in chace of the French,
much inferior to us, who got into Port-Royal on
the 6th, and we returned to Prince Rupert's
Bay on the 7th, having never feen each other,
which occafioned it to be ludicroufly faid by the
people of Dominica, on our return, " that the
" Englifh went on one fide of the ifland, and
" the French on the other, for fear they fhould
" meet."

MAY 9, The ifland of *Défeada*, or *Defiderada*,
(the defireable ifland) the *Santos*, and little ifland
of *Petite-Terre* furrendered to General Barrington,
and on the 14th *Marigalante* fubmitted.

JUNE 3, the fquadron returned to Guadelupe, where the rendezvous of the men of war and tranfports returning to England was fixed at *Baffe-Terre*. On the 15th, the *Rippon* was or-dered to look into Granada, lat. 11°. 45'. N. and on the 17th, difcovered *Monfieur* Du Bom-par lying there, with feven fhips of the line, " Had Commodore Moore, fays DICK, on this " occafion, luckily failed with his whole fquadron " in queft of *Monfieur* Du Bompar, this cam-" paign had glorioufly ended with the DESTRUC-" TION of the FRENCH FLEET in the WEST-IN-" DIES, and the CONQUEST OF GRANADA, which " muft have fallen of courfe."

SOON after this the tranfports, with the troops and convoy, failed for England, and the fquadron for Antigua, where they anchored, June 29. From thence they made Barbadoes, St. Chrifto-pher's, and St. Euftatia. This latter ifland being at this time (1781) a fubject of general converfa-tion, we fhall give Captain MERRY-FELLOW's def-cription of it, in his own words.

" ST. EUSTATIA, is a fmall ifland belonging " to the United Provinces, and lies three " leagues from St *Kitt's*, W. by N. of all the " *Carribees*: it feems the bareft and leaft fertile, " notwithftanding the *Dutch* carry on a very " pwerful trade in the *Weft Indies* from it, and

it

" it has been for many years the market of
" Europe : being poor and naked in itfelf, and
" in all appearance like a ragged rock, it
" thrives by borrowed commodities and a clan-
" deftine traffic with the powers at war ; tranf-
" porting the produce of one enemy to another,
" under the pretence of neutral bottoms. The
" town is badly built, and the houfes very in-
" different; it ftands lofty, and has one hill in
" particular of a very great height, which is
" called *Tumble-down Dick*, and ferves as a land-
" mark at a diftance.

" WHEN the *Rippon* was cruizing off the har-
" bour, there was a *Dutch* man of war, feveral
" *French* privateers, and a great quantity of other
" fhipping lying there. It is an ifland of *fmug-*
" *glers*, and the common receptacle of all the
" *thieves* in Europe. There are feveral forts in
" St. *Euftatia*, and a governor conftantly refides
" there : the prefent one is *Mynheer De Wynd*,
" who is ftiled Governor of St. *Euftatia*, Saba,
" and St. *Martin*'s, though the laft belongs to the
" French."

AFTER touching at Bermuda, or the Summer
Iflands, in N. lat. 32°. 20'. and long. 65°. W.
part of the fleet arrived at Plymouth, Sept. 27,
and the convoy at Spithead, October 5, 1759.
Thus ended an expedition of great importance
to

to the public, in which the *Englifh* arms acquired
a reputation, even from the enemy. Speaking
of the intrepidity and zeal of the officers on this
fervice, and the dangers of climate and mode
of receiving the fire of armed Negroes, lurking
undifcovered behind woods, &c. Dɪ\u0063ᴋ fays, that
the officer commanding, was in the fituation of
Virgil's Rutulian Captain,

> *Sævit atrox* Vᴏʟꜱᴄᴇɴꜱ, *nec teli confpicit ufquàm*
> *Au Ɛtorem, nec quo fe ardens immittere poffit.*
>
> Æn. 9.

But the ᴀᴘᴘʀᴏʙᴀᴛɪᴏɴ of the Sᴏᴠᴇʀᴇɪɢɴ, fays
Dɪ\u0063ᴋ, is the moft ɢʟᴏʀɪᴏᴜꜱ reward a foldier can
acquire!

> Rᴇɢᴇ *incolumi mens omnibus una eft.*

WE cannot conclude this account of our
hero's *Expedition aux Indes Occidentales*, which
he alfo printed in *French*, without adding his
beautiful remark on the treatment of Cᴏʟᴜᴍʙᴜꜱ
by the Europeans, who, after all his difcoveries
nd conquefts, feeing himfelf neglected at court,
on his return to Spain, he retired to *Valladolid*,
where he died of a broken heart, *Anno Dni.* 1506,
aged 64.

> *Por* Caftillo *y por* Leon,
> Itala *Nuevo Monde Halto* Colon.

" Tʜɪꜱ

" THIS GREAT MAN was perhaps the moſt re-
" markable inſtance of diſregarded merit the
" world ever knew; whoſe conſummate know-
" ledge firſt conceived, and whoſe unprece-
" dented courage afterwards executed, deſigns
" and projects beyond all the atchievements of
" the moſt celebrated and illuſtrious conquerors
" amongſt the antients, beyond almoſt the capacity
" and valour of a mortal; launching out into un-
" known ſeas in queſt of an unknown earth, col-
" lecting wealth and riches from kingdoms and
" countries no where heard of; a ſovereign of his
" own creation, who firſt obtained a ſceptre, and
" then found out a world to ſway it in. Variety of
" fortune he endured; at one time loaded with
" honours, at another ſent for home in chains;
" this day HIGH-ADMIRAL of the *Weſtern* ſeas,
" and LORD of all the *Weſtern* globe, the next
" a ſuppliant for mercy, and pleading his cauſe
" for life and liberty; inſulted by his inferiors,
" and diſgraced by his king : then iſſuing forth in
" ſplendor and in power, adding dominion to do-
" minion, and continent to continent; till worn out
" with age and repeated ſervices, he returned to
" *Europe* in a private ſtation, and died univerſally
" regreted and admired, but in the territory of
" the prince he had aggrandized, and the country
" he had enriched *.

---

* *Columbus* was by birth a *Genoeſe*.

" THEN

" THEN at laſt a magnificent monument was
" erected to his memory, the only return made
" him by that ungrateful nation, which derives
" its greateſt influence at this day, from acqui-
" ſitions made by his penetrating mind, and his
" invincible arm : in a word, *Columbus* ſhould only
" have lived in the reign of ſuch a Prince as
" *Alexander*, who wiſhed for nothing ſo much as
" a NEW WORLD to conquer."

Un us Pellœo Juveni non ſufficit orbis
Æſtuat infelix Anguſto limite mundi.

JUV. Sat. 10.

How ſoon after DICK MERRY-FELLOW's arrival
in England did he receive the hand qf Ann,
only daughter of Benjamin Bromhead, Eſq. of
Thurlby near Lincoln, in matrimony, we are
not any where told, but ſuppoſe it to be ſome-
time in the year 1761, as his eldeſt ſon, now
Lieutenant of a Royal Independant Company at
Chatham, was born October 21, 1762.

IN 1761, he raiſed a company of foot at the
breaking out of the Spaniſh war at a great expence, but was not allowed to ſell his company
of marines, a priviledge granted to ſeveral *Scotch*
captains in the marines, and who ſold their com-
panies for a thouſand guineas, at the ſame time
obtaining

obtaining the rank of field-officers, of Major, or Lieutenant-Colonel,

———— No place of office or command,
Not of the greateſt, ſhall be bought or ſold;
Whereas too often honours are confer'd
On ſoldiers and no ſoldiers.

DRYDEN and LEE's Duke of Guiſe.

AT the infamous * peace of Paris, February 10, 1763, his company was reduced in the May following, and he was put upon half-pay.

AFTER this, we imagine DICK retired to Swaffham, a neat and healthy town in Norfolk, where he might enjoy thoſe happy moments of domeſtic felicity inſeperable from the conjugal ſtate, and which he had but lately taſted, though now in his fortieth year. Here alſo, he had time and ſolitude to indulge his paſſion for the muſes, and an opportunity of acquiring ſocial and reſpectable friends : being a man of the world and' a man of letters, his company and converſation was, no doubt, on every occaſion, acceptable : he had learning enough to qualify him for moſt ſpeculative converſation, and experience of mankind ſufficient to direct it with ſucceſs : he was not yet mad enough to follow a <i>fox</i> at the hazard

_____

* DICK's own expreſſion.

of

of his neck, nor bit with the rage for murdering
what is called *Game*, yet he would chearfully
fit down with thofe fons of Actæon, or of Nimrod, " roar a catch," and " fet the table in a
" roar !" nor would he refufe a pint-bumper

To *horfes found, dog's hearty, earths ftopt, and foxes plenty !*

He was what the fraternity efteem—A GOOD
MASON ; and as he was a principal agent in con-
ftituting a lodge, of which he was the *firft*
MASTER, at Swaffham, we fhall fubjoin his own
account of mafonry there.

" In this church was formerly an organ, which
" was broke when the church fell down, but was
" repaired at the fole expence of SIMON BLAKE :
" he alfo gave forty pounds towards erecting a
" new fteeple; and employed, at his own volun-
" tary charge for one whole year, a FREE-MASON
" to re-edify the church : this church is there-
" fore indebted to *free-mafonry* for its prefent
" beauty. The old church fell down in the
" reign of Edward IV. and the new one began
" to be erected about the year 1480, the 20th
" of the fame reign; and by various contribu-
" tions, with the tower at the weft end, was
" finifhed in the year 1510, the firft year of
" Henry VIII. By this it appears that the noble
" art of *free-mafonry* flourifhed in great perfec-
" tion at Swaffham, during the reigns of Ed-
" ward

" ward IV. Edward V. Richard III. Henry VII.
" and Henry VIII.

" It was revived in England with great fplen-
" dor in the reign of GEORGE I. by the Dukes of
" Montague, Buccleugh, and Richmond, under
" whofe patronage very magnificent buildings
" were carried into execution in different parts
" of the kingdom by the extraordinary fkill of
" the fraternity of *free-mafons*; many of whom
" were excellent ARTISTS; and in the year 1764,
" there were no lefs than 328 regular lodges in
" Great-Britain. The art extended itfelf alfo
" to Ireland, where a Grand-mafter was ap-
" pointed, and many of the firft nobility of the
" kingdom prefided, and were members of the
" numerous lodges held in the different counties
" of that kingdom : it flourifhed greatly in
" France, though attempted to be fuppreffed by
" government, but the authority of the king and
" minifters, however abfolute, were ineffectual,
" and *mafonry* triumphs there, and in Ger-
" many to this hour : the King of Puffia is a
" *mafon*, and a powerful patron of this noble
" art."

By MASONS ART th' afpiring dome
In various columns fhall arife;
All climates are their native home,
Their god-like actions reach the fkies.

Chorus.

Chorus.

HEROES *and* KINGS *revere the name,*
Whilft poets fing their lafting fame. .

Great, generous, virtuous, good, and brave,
 Are titles they moft juftly claim ;
Their deeds fhall live beyond the grave,'
 Which fome unborn fhall loud proclaim.

Chorus.

Time fhall their glorious acts inrol,
And LOVE *with* FRIENDSHIP *charm the foul.*

" In the year 1764, *free-mafonry* was revived
" at Swaffham, and the great lodge at the Crown-
" Inn conftituted by authority of the Right
" Honble. Lord Blaney, Lieutenant-General of
" his Majefty's forces, GRAND MASTER of MA-
" SONS, being the 329th lodge in Great Britain.
" Benj. Nuthall, Efq. Alderman of Lynn-Regis,
" was appointed to inftal the new mafter, RICH-
" ARD GARDINER, Efq. and on the 17th of De-
" cember, the day appointed for the inftallation,
" a grand proceffion of *mafons*, confifting of the
" mafter, wardens, and members of the Duke's-
" Head and White-Lion lodges at Lynn, and
" many members of the lodges at Norwich,
" was made from the Crown-Inn to the church
" at eleven o'clock in the morning, where di-
" vine fervice was performed by the Rev. John
" Warren, Rector of Harling, and an excellent
          " fermon

" fermon on the occafion preached by the Rev.
" Charles Chadwick of March in the ifle of
" Ely; after divine fervice the new mafter was
" inftalled with the ufual ceremonies, according
" to the manner of *Mafons*, and an elegant enter-
" tainment was prepared at the Crown. In the
" evening there was a brilliant affembly of
" ladies to celebrate the conftitution of the new
" lodge. In a few months the members of the
" great lodge were cónfiderably encreafed, and
" many of the firft gentlemen of the county were
" admitted into the fraternity.

" The year following, 1765, the Lynn com-
" pany of comedians coming to Swaffham, the
" members of the great lodge were requefted to
" befpeak a play, and on May 6, they befpoke
" the Comedy of Love for Love, which was
" performed to a crowded audience; the mem-
" bers walking in proceffion, properly cloathed,
" to the temporary playhoufe (a barn) where a
" building on the ftage was erected for their
" reception."

The Officers of the Lodge were,

Richard Gardiner, Efq. Master.
William Pawlett, Efq. *Deputy-Mafter.*
William Mafon, Efq. } *Wardens.*
Sir Henry Peyton, Bart.
Sir Clement Trafford, Bart. *Treafurer.*

After

After the play, the following occaſional Epilogue was ſpoken by Mrs. Dyer.

Wrote by the MASTER.

WHILE royal ſplendor, and theatric ſtate,
On Princely BARRY and King GARRICK wait,
How little can we hope our humble ſtage,
Void of all pomp, can your applauſe engage!
For which amongſt you, Ladies, can diſcern
A Covent-Garden in a Swaffham barn? .

Yes, 'tis a Barn—yet fair ones, take me right,
Our's is no Play—we hold a LODGE to night;
And ſhould our building want a ſlight repair,
You ſee we've Friends amongſt the BRETHREN there.
          [Pointing to the *Maſons* on the ſtage.]

Reply the * SCALDS, with MISERABLE frown,
" Maſons repair!—They'd ſooner pull it down—
" A ſet of ranting, roaring, rumbling fellows,
" Who meet to ſing OLD ROSE AND BURN THE BEL-
      LOWS:
" Champaign and claret, dozens in a jerk!
" And then—O Lord! how hard they've been *at work!*

" Next for the SECRET of their own wiſe making,
" HIRAM and BOAZ, and Grand-Maſter JACHIN!
" Poker and tongs! the ſign! the word! the ſtroke!
" 'Tis all a nothing, and 'tis all a joke:
" Nonſenſe on nonſenſe! let them ſtorm and rail,
" Here's the whole hiſt'ry of their MOP and PAIL;

---

* The SCALD-MISERABLE Society,

" For

" For 'tis the fenfe of more than half the Town,
" Their Secret is—a BOTTLE at the *Crown*."

But not fo faft, ye enemies to LIGHT,
I, tho' no Mafon, am their friend to night ;
And, by your leaves, 'tis fomething ftrange, I trow,
To flander that, which none of you can know.
We Women, tho' we like GOOD *Mafons* well,
Sometimes are angry that they will not tell ;
And then we flaunt away from rout to rout,
And fwear, like you, we've found the SECRET out:
But O vain boaft ! to all enquiring eyes,
Too deep the MINE where that bright JEWEL lies !

That Mafons have a SECRET is moft true,
And you, ye Beauties, have a *Secret* too:
Now if the Mafons are fo rigid grown
To keep THEIR Secret to themfelves alone,
Be SILENT in your turns, 'tis that allures,
SILENCE ! and bid the Mafons—find out *your's.*

Thus far conjecture in the comic way,
But let not Fancy lead your thoughts aftray;
The ties of HONOUR only, *Mafons* bind, ·
Friends to each other, and to all mankind :
True to their KING, and for their COUNTRY bold,
They flew to battle, like their Sires of old;
Banifh'd the TROWEL for the barbed fpear, ·
And where loud cannons thunder'd, *form'd the fquare*;
Gallant and gay at MINDEN's glorious plain,
And the proud MORO ftorm'd, alas ! in vain !
In peace, with honeft Hearts they court the fair,
And moft they triumph, when they triumph there :
Their actions known, their bitt'reft foes approve,
For all that *Mafons* afk, is—LOVE for LOVE.

G   THE

" THE noble art of FREE-MASONRY, though
" acknowledged to be very old, was not revived
" in Europe till the feventh century; at which
" time the famous Abbot St. Alban, introduced
" it into England, and firft conftituted a lodge
" at the city of Verulam· (the very fpot where
" the town of St. Alban's in Hertford-fhire now
" ftands) of which he was very fond, and re-
" commended its continuance at his death.

" THE ridiculous focieties of *Bucks, Pande-*
" *monians, Coufins, Antediluvians, Gregorians, Al-*
" *bions, Ubiquitarians, Lumber-troop, Antient-Bri-*
" *tons, Botherems, Free and Eafy,* and a thoufand
" other nonfenfical inftitutions, have fince been
" eftablifhed, either to ferve a party, or in a vain
" imitation of the antient and honourable fociety
" of *Free-Mafons,* which have their day and their
" decline."

O! imitatores, fervum pecus ! HOR.

" And life itfelf's a drama—play'd by fools."

OF Mr. MERRY-FELLOW we have nothing to
record from this time, May 1765, till about
Auguft 1767, when the *natural* diffolution of Parliament had rendered a general election of reprefentatives in Parliament a matter of courfe, the
enfuing fpring. At Lynn-Regis, where DICK
now refided, the " offer of fervices" and a
canvas

canvas had been made fo early as December 12, 1766.

"HITHERTO we have accompanied our hero through thofe viciffitudes of fortune, and variety of character, fo well expreffed in the following lines, on the ærial fcheme of *caftle-building*, a palladium of architecture, of which he was virtually GRAND-MASTER MASON!

" The plodding dull material mortar-man,
" Spends half his life adjufting of his plan ;
" The other half he is perplex'd to find
" Matter and fituation to his mind :"

HE had partook of the fweets of Profperity, and tafted of the bitter cup of Adverfity ! In the prefage of life, he rofe fuperior to his years, and by an eafily-conceived combination of genius and application, gradually acquired a knowledge of the claffics, reputable to thofe feminaries of learning (Eton, Cambridge, and Gottingen) where he ftudied, and very flattering to his friends, but, according to the old adage, " all is not gold that glitters."

No fooner did he enter into the bufy world, than a certain fatality, fometimes merited and fometimes otherwife, attended each action of his life, and feemed to juftify his own remark on his old flame, Mifs-*Fortune*, who contrived to

defeat

defeat him in all his promifed joys. " This,
" fays he, was her ufual trick, having often
" prevented his fuccefs when his hopes moft
" flattered him, by fome *untoward* accident, and
" blafted all his views and defigns, when *neareft*
" the *height* and fummit of enjoyment, fo that
:" he might be faid, in fome meafure, to be like
" the ftone of *Sifyphus*,

—————————ἀλλ' ὅτε μέλλοι

῎ΑΚΡΟΝ ὑπερϐαλέειν, τότ' ἀποςρέψασκε Κραταὶς,
῎Αυτις ἔπειτα πέδονδε Κυλίνδετο Λᾶας ἀναιδής.

ODYSS. L. II.

THUS, fo early as at the age of thirty-one
years, had he a confirmed opinion of that *equi-
voque* of fortune which never forfook him, and at
laft left him " a bankrupt in every thing—but
" experience."

WE have feen him the cloud-capt fop of learning at college, talking of having " *Peripatetic*
" footmen, a *follower* of *Ariftippus* for a *valet de*
" *chambre*, an *Epicurean* cook, with an *Hermetical*
" *Chymift* (who are good only at making fires)
" for a fcullion." Next, he ftruts the heart-
killing *Martinet* of fafhion, who, according to
Shakefpeare, " knows no more of the divifion of
" a battle, than a fpinfter," for mere regimentals

no

no more create a foldier, than the cowl makes a monk.

What knows the ftripling of the foldier's trade,
Beyond his regimentals and cockade?

A fudden tranfition from fcarlet to fable pro-
duces him a fpruce *parfon* of fix-and-twenty, fo
be-powder'd, fo dreffy, fo gallant, and fo vain!

  " I'll be at charges for a looking-glafs,
  " And entertain a fcore or two of taylors
  " To ftudy fafhions to adorn my body."

SHAKESPEARE.

HE was, notwithftanding, a good canonical
in the pulpit and furplice; and although we
cannot contemplate him in a doctor's fcarfe,
pudding-fleeves, ftarched band, and feather-top
grizzle, yet he was not one of thofe irrational
beings who think,

To fpring a covey, or unearth a fox,
In rev'rend fportfmen—is right orthodox.

AGAIN he figures in the *military* line, and not
only tendered his fervices in the field of Mars,
but at the fhrine of Venus.

Beauty was next my theme, and love fincere,
All potent love! whofe influence reigns confeft:—
While bloated wars from pole to pole wide fweep.

G 3 IN

In the republic of letters, òur hero was not leſs
a devotée to fame, than to paſſion ! but

Practice alone muſt form the writer's head,
And ev'ry author to the trade be bred.

Of what the *Reviewers* ſay of Pudica, ſee page
23 of this memoir ; and of his other works, take
the following account.

In the Monthly Catalogue for February 1754,
of the Monthly Review, we find this article
among the poetical. " *An Elegy on the death of*
" *Lady Aſgill*, lady of Sir *Charles Aſgill*, Knight,
" and Alderman of the city of *London*. To
" which is added, an Epitaph on the late Sir
" *Edward Bacon*, Bart. of *Gillingham*, in the
" county of *Norfolk*. By *Richard Gardiner*, Eſq.
" folio, 6d. *Cooper*." The elegy we have never
ſeen, but the epitaph is inſerted in pages 29 and
30 of this memoir.

The Monthly Review of November 1759,
hath " *An Account of the Expedition to the Weſt-*
" *Indies, againſt Martinico, Guadelupe, and other*
" *the Leeward Iſlands ; ſubject to the French King,*
" 1759. By *Richard Gardiner*, Eſq. Captain of
" Marines on board his Majeſty's ſhip *Rippon*,
" on the expedition : 4to. 2s. 6d. *Stuart*."—
with the following ſenſible *critique*.

THE

" The tumult of war has been generally thought moſt unfavourable to the progreſs of literature. Late experience, however, evinces the contrary. During the war in which we are at preſent engaged, the pen has more than kept pace with the ſword; and every ſingle expedition has produced a number of publications. Several military gentlemen, after having ſheathed their ſwords, which they wielded for the honour and ſervice of their country, have brandiſhed their pens for the public information and entertainment. But among the various candidates who have courted reputation in this two-fold capacity of warrior and writer, the martial author of the account now before us, claims pre-eminence in point of erudition. This very ſprightly and learned piece is ſo profuſely embelliſhed with claſſical decorations, that it is very difficult to diſcover the ground of the work, for the thickneſs of the embroidery. We Reviewers, however, who are not dazzled by the brilliance of quotation, endeavour to do juſtice to an author's intrinſic merit, abſtracted from his borrowed ornaments.

" When we conſider the profeſſed deſign of this performance, we are concerned to ſay, that the writer does not ſeem to have ſucceeded in the execution. His preface informs us, that " the " deſign of ſubmitting to the public the follow-
" ing

" ing fheets, is principally owing to a variety
- " of afperfions thrown out upon the *Britifb officers*
" employed on this expedition.—Some," he continues, " cried out vehemently againft the retreat
" of the troops from MARTINICO, whilft others
" as loudly exclaimed againft the capitulation of
" Guadelupe.—It was, therefore," he concludes,
" in regard to thefe virulences, that he became
" determined to draw a little account of all the
" material movements of the fleets and forces,"
&c. &c.

" THIS intent is, no doubt, laudable. But
how does this little account remove the virulences ; efpecially with regard to the retreat from
Martinico? after having defcribed the efforts
made for the reduction of that ifland, and the
promifing appearance of fuccefs, which flattered
the troops with a fpeedy conqueft of the metropolis, in the very next paragraph the writer
fubjoins, that General Hopfon fent to acquaint
the Commodore, that he found it impoffible to
ftand his ground, unlefs the fquadron could give
him affiftance, by landing fome heavy cannon, &c,
at the Savanna ; or, that the Commodore would
attack the Citadel in the Bay, at the fame time
he did it on the fhore ; both which, he adds,
were judged to be impracticable ; upon which
the General re-imbarked.

HERE

" Here, however, we naturally look for reafons why it became impoffible for the General
to maintain his ground, after fuch flattering appearance of fuccefs : and if any virulences have
been vented, on account of the retreat, they certainly will never be removed by barely repeating
the fact, without an attempt to juftify the pro-
ceeding.

" Nevertheless, this writer, though not con-
clufive in point of argument, is fpecious, and not
unentertaining. He appears to have a lively
imagination, and his ftile, though too flippant for
the fubject, is free and fprightly. It would be
injuftice not to acknowledge, that there is fomething picturefque in his imagery, of which the
following defcription of the appearance of Barbadoes, may ferve as a fpecimen.

" As the fhips approached, the ifland rofe
" gradually out of the fea, with a delightful
" verdure, prefenting a moft inviting profpect of
" the country all around, which looked like a
" garden; the plantations were amazingly beau-
" tiful, interfperfed at little diftances from each
" other, and adorned with fruits of various co-
" lours; fome were fpread out in fine open
" lawns, in others the waving canes bowed
" gently to the wind, from hanging mountains,
" while the continual motion of the fugar-mills,
difperfed

" difperfed in every part, and working, as it
" were, in concert, enlivened the engaging fcene,
" and made it infinitely ftriking to eyes long
" accuftomed to the unentertaining range of fky
" and water only."

UPON DICK's leaving the amphibious fervice
of *Marine*, and entering again into the foot, he
facrificed in the temple of Hymen to the god of
love, and became *the married man*, though no
Benediƈine.

SUBTLE irony and keen fatire was his *forte*,
in which he was fublimely liberal, and we have
feen this unfortunate fon of Apollo, mounted on
Pegafus, ride full fpeed up *Parnaffus*, brandifhing
the barbed fpear of defamatory fatire o'er the
heads of a hoft of adverfaries, each trembling
as

" The wretch, with not a virtue of his own,"

which, like the eel, a non-generant, fprang up
from the dirt and filth thrown from him. .

AND now, having brought our hero into the
political zone, we fhall proclaim him a PATRIOT!
of the firft water;—in the zenith of his confequence, and fo

> Politic, as if one eye,
> Upon the other was a fpy.

IN

In the contefted election for the borough of
Lynn-Regis, and for the county of Norfolk, 1768,
Dick Merry-fellow readily embraced what
is called *the country intereft*, and entered heartily
into the bufinefs of declamation and abufe;—
weapons now fo hacked as to loofe their edge,.

" His faws were toothlefs, and his hatchets lead,"

It is not to be expected that we fhould follow the
candidates, or their adherents, through the multi-
plicity of electioneering advertifements, fquibs,
reafons, ftrictures, queries, anfwers, &c. publifhed
on the occafion, nor fwell this memoir with a minute detail of tranfactions; for, we agree with an
author who fays, " *a great book is a great evil*;"
our chief intention being to preferve the fongs,
epigrams, &c. wrote by our hero; in doing which,
we mean no offence to the parties:—truth,
and the nature of our prefent work, obliges us
to render this—*a Repofitory of all his metrical compofitions,*

By " the Lynn Magazine; or a collection
" of papers, publifhed during the conteft in that
" town,"

" *Undique Clamor Tollitur.*

Virg."

we

we find, that the candidates and ftate of the
poll were as follows,

The Honble. Tho. Walpole of London   200
Sir John Turner, Bart. of Warham   —   174
Crifp Molineux, Efq. of Garboldifham   159

whereupon the two former were declared duly
elected, March 21, 1768. In 1774, Sir John
Turner declined offering himfelf, and Mr. Molineux was chofen along with Mr. Walpole; and
again in 1780.

At the time of this conteft, the legality or
illegality of GENERAL WARRANTS * was the political hobby-horfe, and the criterion of political
principles: of this the writers on either fide
availed themfelves, and decided on its merits,
even before that very important queftion came
before Parliament, or the gentlemen of the long-
robe in Weftminfter-hall. DICK MERRY-FELLOW
was a declared enemy to every member or candidate, who had been, in any fhape, an advocate
for the *arbitrary* and *unconftitutional* power of the
Star-chamber; as alfo to the adminiftration of
Lord *Bute*; but whether this averfion to the
Scots *Premier*, arofe from fentiments of true pa-
triotifm, or the circumftance of DICK's narrow

---

* General Warrants were publicly burnt at Lynn-regis, in
1765, John Cary, Efq. Mayor.

efcape

efcape from being trampled on by the horfes and carriage of that nobleman, we will not take upon us to determine; but certain it is, that DICK gave the coachman the following mild rebuke.

Drive on, friend John! all envy thee thy ftation,
Since thou drives him—who drives the K—g and nation.

DICK having thus thrown down the gauntlet, as the avowed champion of the *country intereft*, no wonder that we find him fo much neglected by the *Court*, with refpect to military preferments; and this conduct of adminiftration, we are bold to fay, hath deprived Great Britain of the fervices of many able officers, and created many warm oppofitionifts, both in and out of Parliament.

ALONG with the torrent of abufe and calumny that overwhelms the plains of decorum and free-dom of election, a *ftony* truth will now and then tumble forward with the current, and make its way to the feelings and judgment of the honeft electors;—for *truth* is pleafing in any drefs:

Mille habet ornatus, mille decenter habet.

AGREEABLE to our plan, we fhall pafs over the addreffes, letters, replies, rejoinders, &c. and be-gin our poetical farrago, with

The

The CASE of the Honourable LYNN MERCHANT,
moſt circumſtantially ſtated : .

By a Friend.

THE *Creoles* all grieve that their friend *Jemmy Spitter**
. Has lately been put in a *damnable* twitter,
For the loſs of his *plumbs* and *onions* from *port*,
Which, among the *Lynn* wits, makes excellent ſport.
Demand on demand he made for his *onions*,
The land-waiters humm'd him, thoſe ſaucy *raſcallions*,
He then *condeſcended* to the *Dep. Col.* to write,
The Dep. condeſcended—no reply to indite.
Jemmy then ſent *reproaches* for want of behaviour
To a merchant ſo *potent*—ſo full of—pallaver—
With his *plumbs* he had plann'd th' wives palates to pleaſe
Of M-l-n—x *freemen*—day nor night had he eaſe—
He *dreamt* of his *plumbs*—in his dreams gave direction
To diſperſe the *ſweet boxes* to his friends of election.
He propos'd a ſnug treat to theſe M-l-n—x *honies*,
And wanted his *onions* to ſmother ſome *Conies*,
He waited and waited 'till the rabbits grew ſtale,
So now is determin'd to give *beef* and S*tar ale*, }
And tiff'd out in his *Spencer* to tell his ſad tale. }
How wretched and reſtleſs, *thrice* he ſent to V A N-
        COUVER,†
That *little vagary—harlequino* all over—
What meant you *Dep. Col?*—to eat all his *plumbs?*
Zounds!—VAN—were they mine, I'd cut off—-your
        thumbs,

---

* Mr. James F-ſh, the Merchant.
† Deputy Collector of the port of *L-nn-R-g-s.*

Nay

Nay, your legs too to boot, for your giving no anſwer,
I'd ſpoil you for ever from being a *dancer*—
Jemmy farther declares—tho' the *duty* be offer'd,
And full eighteen-pence conſcientiouſly proffer'd,
Inſtead of receiving this *duty* for *King,* Sir !
They gave only a *protracting*, *evaſive*, ſly *anſwer.*
Jemmy Spitter thus *piqu'd*, and no *plumbs* could he get,
Well might his eyes twinkle, and he foam in ſuch pet.
But the worſt's ſtill to come—tho' he wrote to the Board,
For theſe *plumbs* and theſe *onions*—there's not come a
    word
Of the leaſt ſatisfaction—no more than from V AN—
This ſtroke's then a proof—what they *think* of the *man.*

L y n n, *July* 11, 1767.

The above paper is a feeble attempt to ridicule a memorial delivered in to the Commiſſioners
of the Cuſtoms, by an eminent *Lynn* Merchant,
complaining of an unjuſt ſeizure at the port of
Lynn; but the poetaſter, whoever he was, ſinks
far beneath the weight of the following pen,
which, we doubt not, was D i c k's.

N. B. We have inſerted the former merely to
ſet off the latter.

On reading a late *Poetical Publication* at the
                    Cuſtom-Houſe.

N O W, by St. Paul ! as Richard ſwore of old,
    True ſterling wit exceeds true ſterling gold :
Verſe from the *Cuſtom-houſe !* ſee, townſmen, ſee !
And what is ſtranger ſtill—'tis *duty free:*

All

All given gratis to each foul who enters,
And ready as the coin that pays debentures:
No more fhall party-feuds diftract our town,
Thefe lines fhall beat all oppofition down.
No more that grating found to T-RN-R's ears,
The name of M-L-N--X, alarm our fears:
No longer wanted in the ftreets to Hector.
Sir J-HN's great bulwark ftrut, the great C-ll-B-r;*
While little VAN his happy ftars fhall blefs,
And not one foul fhall wifh him to be lefs:
Ev'n GEORGE † pacific grows, and fhall he fpit,
It fhan't be venom, but it fhall be wit;
GEORGE, who, at all times, truth alone has fpoke,
Ne'er forfeited his word, nor promife broke.
W-LP-LE fhall poll, and willing freemen vote,
And, not a M-L-N--X fhall change his note;
All parties fhall alike admire the ftrain,
And F-SH ‡ fhall prefs the bard to write again:
Bleft poet! who fo early could affuage
All private rancor, and all public rage,
To thee the peace of this great town we owe,
Who made the pride of T-RN-R ftoop fo low.

LYNN, *July* 16, 1767.

---

* Ch-rl-s T-rn-r, Efq. brother to Sir J-hn, and Mayor at
the election.

† Mr. G—rge H-gge, a wealthy merchant of *L-nn R-g-s*.

‡ This gentleman was fo remarkable for the fingularity of
his temper and actions, that he was generally called, *an Odd
Fyfh*.

To

To the H-gh-Sh—r-ff.*

EPIGRAM.

NO ! your coach, Mr. *Sheriff*, now the *Treafury*'s gone;
Inftead of WILL. M-xs-N, may ferve poor Sir J-HN.
And O ! what a fall ! how is grandeur incog,
When the T-RN-RS bow down, at the foot of a H-G !

LYNN, *July* 26, 1767.

———————————————

The Adventures of TRISTRAM SHANDY, *Auguft* 31,
1767.

— — — — — — — — — — — — — — —
— — — — — — fo as we were riding over the marfhes,
a good round trot, *Simpkin* firft, I, of courfe, following;
I happened to be ruminating on fome domeftic affairs of
my own, my right hand loofely holding the bridle, and
my wife *Dulcia's* new-lafhed hand-whip, my left bearing
upon the faddle, to prevent its chaffing my fcarlet velvet
breeches, with my eyes fixed on my left foot, which had
the filver-ftuded fpur on, to protect *Dapper* from the penetration of that unweildy weapon ; when, with a fudden
jerk, *Simpkin* ftopped his *Ruby* : *Dapper* being clofe to
Ruby, and not aware of the ftop, ran her head againft
his flourifhing tail ; which fo irritated him, that he kicked
Dapper over the cheft, and flung neighbour *Simpkin out*
of his faddle *into* the dirt : *Dapper*, receiving fo unexpected
a blow, turned fhort off to the right, and caufed me, vo-
luntarily, to ftick the rowels of the fpur into her fide;

———————————————

* C—p M—x, Efq. of G—m.

H   no

no fooner did fhe feel a fmart fo uncommon to her, than
fhe fet off, galloping, kicking, f--t--g, &c. and notwithftanding I let fall the reins and the new-lafhed whip, and
clung faft to the mane and the faddle pommel, I rode
not ten yards, before the fcarlet velvet breeches were
rent open between the legs to fuch a degree that -   -
- - - - - - - - - - - - - : well,—I was fo
frightened, that I let go my hold and fell plump into a
ditch, as wide and as deep as that which Mrs. *Flouncer*
calls the hoh ! hoh ! at the bottom of 'Squire *Randolph*'s
terrace-walk. By that time I had crept out of my cold
bath, neighbour *Simpkin* had remounted *Ruby*, having
only the addition of a little dirt on the back fkirt of his
coat, &c. But, O ! ye gods, that prefide over the dirty
roads of MARSHLAND, defend me from fuch another
fatality !——Well, neighbour *Simpkin* found my whip,
(though the lafh was a little daubed) catched *Dapper*, and
after I had pulled off that curfed fpur, I mounted again,
draggled as I was, fcarce knowing whether I was male
or female, but by the flit - - - - - . As we jogged
on, pray, neighbour, (fays I) what might be the occafion of
that fudden ftop, which has proved fo unlucky to us
both ?—look ! *Triftram*, look ! fays he, feeming to recollect himfelf, fee yonder how the ftreamers fly at the
top-mafts heads !—then, clapping fpurs to *Ruby*, he rode
furioufly forward, without giving me time to anfwer.
- - - - - - - - - - - - Be fure, mafter
Buckram, that you mend the flit in my fcarlet velvet
breeches judicioufly; " Sir," fays the taylor, fetting his
arms a-kimbo, " I am a *freeman*, and work for the CAN-
DIDATES, and furely I can ftop a flit."

- - - - - - - - - - - - - - - -

There's

There's great rejoicing in town to day; pray what may be the reaſon? " Reaſon!" ſays the landlord, ſhaking his head, " I ſee no reaſon in it, neither do others that ſee at all; ſome rejoice through *prepoſſeſſion*, others through *oppoſi-tion*; ſome take a ſerpent by the head (forgetting the ſting) to annoy others with the tail : but if you walk down to the water-ſide, near the place where you landed, you will ſee ſuch a ſcene of ſtupidity, abſurdity—well, God pre-ſerve us from arbitrators and arbitration!"—Away went I, as directed by the landlord, not doubting but I ſhould find neighbour *Simpkin* amongſt the *rabble*; I was right, there was he in the midſt of them, aboard of a ſhip lying a-long-ſide of the quay, dirty as he was, (though by the bye, there were others there as *dirty* as himſelf) : ſo I thought I would ſee what they were doing aſhore before I went aboard. - - - - - - - - - - - -

- - What are thoſe caſks there ?—" O Sir," ſays the woman, " *Sir* JOHN and his friends, God bleſs them! are giving away *ale* to his friends and well-wiſhers."— " Avaſt! avaſt! you d—n'd lying b—h," ſays a ſailor, who lay with his legs and arms extended on a piece of timber, " d—mn *Sir* JOHN and his friends, I ſay!—ale? ſmall beer and jalap.—Freemen?—ſlaves! ſlaves! not Engliſhmen, Scotſmen, d—mn 'em, *Scotſmen!—well-wiſher?*—no, no, I can contradict that; for I myſelf would ſteer him in a cockle-boat a thouſand leagues to ſea, if I might then have the pleaſure of—O the gripes!—Damn GENERAL WARRANTS," ſays he, jumping up and running to a convenient corner, in order to join ſeveral others who were diſcharging *Sir* JOHN's benevolence in a rather un-ſeemly manner; and as I advanced towards the ſhip I ſcarce ſaw any thing but diſtorted features; occaſioned, I ſuppoſe, by the inteſtine commotions which the particles

H 2   of

of air conveyed into the *abdomen* with each draught of the
yet fermenting liquor, had excited, and my ears were con-
tinually faluted with the confufed exclamations of " M-
l-n-x *for ever!*—d-mn *Sir* JOHN and his *belch!*"—*Sir*
JOHN? *Sir* JOHN? cried I to myfelf, feeling whether all
were right about the breeches (forgetting that they were
my landlord's beft buckfkin) as I was going aboard, for I
was willing to go decently, how far foever I might ac-
quiefce with the abfurdities of the reft when there. - -
- - - - - - - - - - - - - So, neighbour
Simpkin, you outride me, and to fome purpofe, if one may
judge of things by *outward* appearances. " Hufh! hufh!"
fays he, " that is *Sir* GEORGE:" *Sir* GEORGE? *Sir*
GEORGE? fays I: why, the devil is in the people fure!—
nothing but *Sir* JOHN afhore, and *Sir* GEORGE aboard;
why fure, a *Quixotical* fpirit has poffeffed them, and turned
them all into knights and baronets!—" Sir," fays the
man, who fat on the capftern, " if you will be a filent
fpectator with me, and attend to their difcourfe, you'll
foon find the occafion of this *ridiculous meeting*. - - -
- - - - - - - - - Come, I'll give you a toaft;
here's the *M-y-r el-Ct!*" and why not the *M-y-r-ft*
too? fays I to my friend. " Softly!" fays he, " there is
none, the *M-y-r el-Ct* keeps * * *"—*We* have the
majority already, fays *Sir* GEORGE :—" The minority, I'm
fure then," fays my friend to me; " for whatever he
affirms *to be*, is ever found *not to be :*"—Oh! ho! this is
electioneering in every *bad* fenfe of the word, fays I, jumping off the capftern and walking afhore. - - - -
- - - - - - - - - - - - - - - -
Your fervant, Mr. *Simpkin!* hey! hey! what, neither
drunk nor mad?—" Neither" fays he; " the diftemper
that raged aboard was not contagious, at leaft it did not
affect

affect me any longer than while I bore a part in the action:" Well then, fays I, I'll fend to know whether the fcarlet velvet breeches are mended, and in the mean time I'll give you the reigning topic of thofe people in the kitchen.—They all agree that *Sir* John did not act with honour. " But what is honour?" fays anpther; fo honour ran throughout the whole affembly undefined ; at laft, up ftarts a gardener, and faid " he knew what *fupported* honour; and he believed, *Sir* John's honour:" " What? what?" fays the reft of the affembly ; " vegetables," " fays he: " for an Englifhman is a *fcurvy* fellow unlefs he eats vegetables ; now a *pea* is a vegetable, therefore I affirm a *pea* to be a *part* of the fupport." Then up jumps a taylor, and urged " that trade, generally fpeaking, fupported Englifh honour ; and in ours, added he, honour is entirely relied on ; therefore," putting my-felf in *Sir* John's ftead, " if I can, for a yard, charge *an ell* with impunity, it is the *ell*, gentlemen, the *ell* that is a material fupport of my honour in the world." " Silence! filence !" fays a fhabby-looking fellow, who was playing at *All-fours* with another in a corner of the room, " all ftatefmen and gamblers!—rank gamblers! gentlemen—now we are ftatefmen," fays he to his partner, " playing for * * * *, you are eight" " fo am I,"—" hearts is trumps, *and the knave is turned up*"—" play away"—" there's the king ;" " aye, but there's the *ace*—now I infift upon this *ace's* fupporting my honour, I can *play again.*"—So I fummed up their opinions on the fupport of that honour which actuated *Sir* John, juft in the manner I took them down during the debate, thus,

H 3

The

The *Gardener* - - -   *A* P
The *Taylor* - - - :   L
The *Gamefter* an - - -   A C E.

Total - - - . *A* PLACE.

" So, as the fcarlet velvet breeches were juft come from the taylor's, I wifhed neighbour *Simpkin* a good night.",

THIS ADVENTURE flowed from the lively pen of DICK MERRY-FELLOW, and is replete with vigorous traits of the *Shandian* portray, .The incidents are well-woven, and the circumftance of the *rent breeches* natural ; though the whole ftory is founded only on Mr. G—— H-gge's giving a barrel or two of beer to the populous on board one of his own fhips in the harbour. The political fatire is ingenious and truly comic, and the critical analyzation of *A* PLACE is figurative and humorous; and though this *bagatelle* be incongruous with our avowed intention of not inferting *profaic* effays, we could not refift the temptation of admitting it.

EPIGRAM upon the TIMES.

I.

WHEN M-L-N—x came firft to town,
With colours and what not ;'
" See ! where the rebels come, fee there !"
Exclaims an angry *Scot,*

II.

II.

" Rebels, quoth *John*, I've often feen .
    " At *Tyburn* where they hung 'em ;
" Why, *Sawney*, look ! in all this crowd
    " There's ne'er a *Scot* among 'em."

To the AUTHOR *of the* EPIGRAM, *addreſſed to*
RICHARD MERRY-FELLOW, *Eſq. accuſing*
him of poverty. Dated Lynn-Regis.

O Force of poignant fatire ! known before :
    'Tis granted, RICHARD MERRY-FELLOW'S *poor:*
Of fortune's gifts, he never made his boaſt,
He never *ſmuggled* on the N-rf-lk coaſt :
He ne'er by rapine made his road to gold,
No pariſh *church-rates* in his coffers roll'd,   }
Nor for a *crown* his brother's honor fold :
Sign'd no *debentures*, then, foul deed of ſhame !
Implored his fervant to *eraſe* his name.
Oppreſſion, ruin, never mark'd his way,
He left to grow the LETTICE * of the day :
No hoards by fraud of every kind acquir'd,
Each honeſt heart with indignation fir'd :
No injur'd innocents who beg their bread,
- Loud, as he walks, vent curſes on his head :
Around, and unappall'd he caſts his eye,
By him no widows ſtarve, no orphans cry ;

---

* Mr. Lettice, a merchant at Lynn —" how could it be
" otherwiſe ? was it poſſible for a *Lettice* to take root under
" the noſe of a *H-g*.

By foul extortion fqueez'd he fcorns all wealth,
Yet lives in fpirits, and yet lives in health :
Poor tho' he was, he ne'er refus'd to lend
In time of need ten ducats to a friend ;
A * noble friend! pattern to peers alive !
Who but three days before denied him——five.
By no vile arts encreas'd his fcanty ftore ;
What SOLDIER ever blufh'd for being *poor* ?
Who ferves his country, acts the nobleft part,
He's rich enough who has an HONEST HEART,

Yet ftand aloof! ye flaves! ye venal tribe !
Whom T-RN-R *bullies*, and whom H-GGE can *bribe* !
H-GGE ! that mean wretch, whofe dirt-collected bags
Arofe ftom *gaping cockles* fold in *rags* :
Down to thy dunghill, *muckworm*, and be dumb !
Thou fon of infamy, tho' worth a plumb !
All ranks fhall fcorn thee, moft when in thy pride,
That is, when Sir J-HN T-RN-R's by thy fide.
The mufe, though *poor*, that mongrel herd difdains,
Who cringe to tryants, and who covet chains ;
Who, meanly paffive, in one fatal hour
May doom themfelves and children, flaves to pow'r ;
Cowards ! too bafe to form the patriot ftand !
And facrifice to *thieves* their native land.

LYNN, Dec. 11, 1767.

* Lord T——, at the Hotel de Flandres, April, 1744.

A.

A New Song, fung at Mr. W-lp-le's meeting at the Crown-tavern in *King's-Lynn*, on Thurf-day, February 25, 1768.

I.

COME, cheer up my boys! and to liberty fing,
To W-lp-le and O-f--d, true friends to the *King* :
Let party-diftinctions raife up or pull down,
Here's a health to the *king*, and his friends to the *crown*.
Hearts of oak are we ftill, and true honeft men,
We always are ready,
Steady, boys, fteady,
And a W-lp-le, *a* W-lp le *fhall ever be in*.

II.

When W-lp-le, a name to this town ever dear,
Shall have gain'd his election, and rides in the chair ;
Our choice will have fhewn what true Britons fhould be,
Our choice will have fhewn that Lynn dares to be *free*.
Hearts of oak are we ftill, &c.

III.

When party ran high, in the reign of the *Queen*,
And *Jemmy's* ftaunch friends at the council were feen ;
Sir Robert ftepp'd forth, to the honour of Lynn,
And King George he foon after in triumph brought in.
Hearts of oak are we ftill, &c.

IV.

May Gr-ft-n long flourifh the nation's delight!
Boafts the crown of *Old England*, a jewel more bright ?
May

May the tools, of oppreffion be all kept in awe,
And C-MBDEN prefide at the head of the law!
Hearts of aak are we ftill, &c.

V.

From WILLIAM the *Norman*, from JOHN, *King of* LYNN,
Who gave us our *Charter*, we *Free-men* have been ;
We are true to our *king*, yet will fight for our *laws*,
And will cheerfully *die* in *our country's* caufe.
Hearts of oak are we ftill, &c.

VI.

Come, fill up a bumper, and round let us ftand ;
Old England's our toaft, take your glaffes in hand ;
May *loyalty*, *liberty*, flourifh in LYNN,
And a W-LP-LE, a W-LP-LE for *ever* be in.
Hearts of oak are we ftill, &c.

LYNN-REGIS, *Feb.* 25, 1768.

On a moft extraordinary PROTEST made on *February* 15, 1768, at the time a writ of Mandamus was ferved by Mr. *Carlos C-ny*, Attorney, on the Mayor and members of the corporation, for having refufed *William Peacock*, the younger, his *freedom*.

STRANGE contradiction ! how *protefters* vary,
From AL--RS-N the gruff, to driv'ling C-RY.
This *very man* for whom they make fuch rout,
Years fince they fet afide and voted out—

The

The very *Cafe* now wrong, before was right,
And that iruft now be black which then was white ;
Your *point* by this Mandamus you'll ne'er reach,
So, *good Don* CARLOS, * with it wipe your breech.

LYNN, *Feb.* 25, 1768.

The KING's BENCH *Mufic*, or the WESTMINSTER *Hornpipe*.

YE ! idle triflers of the prefent day !
   Ye ! *printer's devils*, flaves to *George's* pay !
Ye ! *knights* and *doctors !* who *correct* the prefs,
And make yourfelves, though little, yet look lefs !
CARLOS, long us'd your malice to difdain,
From profe or verfe feels not a moment's pain ;
He boafts no *privilege*, wants no *protection*,
Sneaks to no *coufins—bribes* for no election :
Mandamus-arm'd, Lord MANSFIELD in his hand,
He enters boldly, bids *oppreffion* ftand :
Twelve freedoms ftrait attends his juft requeft,
W LP-LE and CRISP got twelve, Sir JOHN—the reft ;
The mayor turns pale and trembles at the *hall :*
For *fal volatile* the Serjeants call !
While confcious virtue, with diftinguifh'd grace,
Sits ever fmiling on the brow of C-SE.
See ! CARLOS laughs, Sir JOHN looks grave and *fnuffs*,
The *Doctor* quibbles, half-bred *Jemmy* huffs:
The Doctor *quibbles !* that I never heard ;
FR--M-N.avers, he cannot—break *his word.*

---

* Mr. Carlos C-ny,.commonly called *Lawyer* C-ny.

Tag's

Tags all abroad ! Sir GEORGE is at a ſtand !
Then ſends for comfort to *ſagacious* BL-ND :
A-DL-Y's *lack-luſtre* eye completes the ſcene
He takes a leſſon, to divert his ſpleen,
Of *Polly* V—NC—T, his dear *dancing queen.*

O ! Doctor, Doctor, let the preſs alone,
And do not *firſt* begin to *throw*—a ſtone ;
To GEORGE and H-M-LT-N * the types reſign,
GARRET's † beſt friends ! and let true *genius* ſhine.

LYNN-REGIS, *Feb.* 26, 1768.

A CHARACTER.

LONG tainted with a luſtful goût,
And long indulg'd with *J-nn-y* too !
A brazen front—and figure trim,
A perfect ſpruce—in air and whim ;
Conceited—to a high degree,
Flippant—abſurd—diſguſtful free :
Affecting knowledge—vain pretence !
Without the dawn of common-ſenſe ;
To other's merit—wilful blind,
To his dear ſelf—how vaſtly kind !
Nay, loves his punk ſo very much,
None but himſelf * * * * * * * muſt touch ;
" Right *Seignior Gliſter*—who ſo true
" Could fix the pipe, and ſquirt it too ?
" 'Twas kindly done—your *J-nn-y*, ſure,
" Muſt love you long for ſuch a cure."
                                        PASQUIN.
LYNN-REGIS, *Feb.* 29, 1768.

---

† Scots Phyſician,   * Printer,

As

As you Like it ! *addreſſed to the* Author *of the* CHARACTER.

O! PARTY what a merry *queen* art thou?
Poets to make of *pipers*, heav'n knows 'how!
For tho' the *Doctor's* much inclin'd to hear,
The *Caledonian hum* ſtill grates his ear.
Sweet muſic travels, and the *waits* go round,
O ! ſhould they play on ſome *forbidden* ground !
Name it not, ye *chaſte* ſtars ! *chaſte* T-RN-R cries;
Then dabs with *luſtre*-water A-DL-Y's eyes.

If SWIFT of *nice* men true deſcription gives,
Our poet is the *niceſt* man that lives:
And what to prove the definition true
Will more amaze you, he's a *Scots-man* too !
Who from his window never yet ſent down
God's gifts, at ſecond-hand, to *cleanſe* the town.
But papers in his hair, ſo ſpruce and prim,
Steals out to take a peep at *Jenny's Whim*.*

Doctor ! Sir J-HN ! ye B-TE-directed bands !
'Tis time to change, and alſo *waſh* your hands:
Sir GEORGE's poets ! ye white-liver'd crew !
CARLOS ſtill laughs, and more, ſtill laughs at you:
He ſtole no *cockles*, and he never ſmuggled;
Cring'd to no *Scot*, nor, Scot-like, trick'd and juggled :
He robb'd no *couſins*, *plunder'd no man's heir*,
His heart is eaſy, and his honour clear.

LYNN-REGIS, *March* 1, 1768,

---

* A place of public entertainment near Chelſea.

The

The C O U N C I L.

Confedere duces et vulgi ftanti corona furgit ad hos—

A LL hands were pip'd : to them up rofe Sir J--N,
With eye dejected, and with vifage wan :
" Friends ! tradefmen ! bl-cks ! you who through thick
    and thin,
" Dafh deep and muddy all, *to bring me in*;
" What thanks your zeal and ardor fhall repay,
" Should fortune fmile on that aufpicious day,
" When *fweet* oppreffion claims your patriot aid,
" And LAW and LIBERTY fhall low be laid ;
" Lo ! *Magna Charta;* bubble in the air,
" Blown by old fools to make young madmen ftare !
" Afk deep-read W-DEH--SE*, or his *wifdom* B-C-N*,
" They'll tell you GENERAL WARRANTS were *miftaken*;
" They're *conftitutional,* and ufeful things
" To make good fubjects to good Britifh kings :
" Or, if authority you want ftill better,
" Afk the *true-blue fcribe* of B-XT-N's letter.
" What faid DE G--Y, your *freeman* at the hall ? †
" That *you were wrong,* he told you, *one* and *all:*
" *Your cry was* LIBERTY he knew full well ;
" But what it was—*not one of you* could tell ;
" Ev'n ftamp-act T--NSH--D, *cyder-barrel* P--R,
" Safe from Qu-B-C, and now no danger near,
" Will roar for B-TE and *pow'r* from morn till night,
" And challenge you—unlefs *he knows* you'll fight.

" *Paffive-obedience* to the rule of kings
" And *minifters,* alone true quiet brings :

---

* Members who voted in favor of general warrants,
† September 29, 1767.

" Does

" Does it to rabble or to mob belong
" To hold difcourfe of what is *right* or *wrong* ?
" To defcant on what fuits the common weal
" As they fhall reafon, and as they fhall feel ?
" Grant me fuccefs, ye heav'ns! but on the day,
" I'll teach the *ragged cafuifts* to *obey.*
" Shall *freemen* vile, *prefume* our thoughts to fcan ;
" From *outward* actions judge of *inward* man ?
" Shall *Robin* BODHAM all our projects fmoke,
" And *Pefcod* cut his *dry* licentious joke ?
" Shall ftubborn *Crifpin* to his promife hold
" Full *twenty pieces well* and *truly* told ?
" O ! for a rod of iron to take down
" Each faucy knave that meets me with a frown !
" Who from his ftall moft impudently breaks,
" And keeps his *hat on*—while to me he fpeaks !
" Where is the arm of pow'r ? for that's my plan :
" Without *defpotic power*, what is man ?"
He ceas'd : his fpeech for approbation call'd ;
GEORGE fmirk'd—CL-RKE cock'd his chin—and ELS-
D-N fquall'd.

But not fo M-X-Y ALL-N ; he abhorr'd
Oppreffion, tho' he found it in a lord.
" Sir J-HN," fays he, " that we are fomewhat *mir'd*,
" Have waded through *bad* roads till we are tir'd,
" (Shame to us all) I own it is moft true ;
" But who could think, to hear it, Sir, from you ?
" Nay, do not frown at me, for I'm not hurt ;
" I fay, you brought us into all this dirt.
" I hate oppreffion, I deteft your plan
" Of pow'r, and fo muft ev'ry *honeft* man.
" Yon call us *Bl—cks*, but I the fact deny ;
" Sir GEORGE may be your *Bl—ck*, Sir, but not I."

" O

" O yes !" cries Sir GEORGE, and gives a fudden ftart;
" I'll be your *Bl—ck*, Sir J-HN, with all my heart.
" BUCKHORSE and I (for I fhall bring him down)
" Will *grub* in ev'ry fink-hole of the town :
" We'll do your bufinefs for you in a trice;
" I hate fuch friends who are—fo very nice :
" Let 'em fay what they will, let GARDINER write;
" Let Ev—R—RD fing, and F—sH and C—RY bite;
" I put no value on an *empty name*,
" BUCKHORSE and I—*feel* pretty much the fame."
He fpoke, loud peals of laughter rend the air,
The Council rofe, and *Lawlefs* left the chair ;
Smil'd *to himfelf*, as near obfervers tell,
But fwore Lord CHATAAM ne'er fpoke *half fo well*.

In times of yore, e'er he became fo big,
GEORGE was, we all muft own, a *pretty pig*;
Till fortune, dame capricious, and wild chance,
Sent him to Paris——there to learn to dance.
He hunted with the *King*, the *King* admired,
And the firft *princes* of the *blood* retired.
In rapture GEORGE replough'd the azure main,
Jack-boots, *bag-wig*, and hat of *pointe-d' Efpagne :*
Down *Chequer-Street* he prances in his *geers*;
Old *Glout* beheld and——*pull'd him by the ears.*

Did ever *genuis*, returning home,
Exalted and improv'd, from *Greece* or *Rome*,
Endure a fhock like this? he died away !
His foreign trinkets and his *French* array,
Shatter'd and fhiver'd all, in one fhort hour !
The dire effects of arbitrary pow'r !

LYNN-REGIS, *Feb.* 15, 1768.

THIS

*T*HIS laſt poem is not diſgraceful to DICK's
muſe, who, we muſt acknowledge, oft times
from the attic deſcended to the ſcullery, where
being drudge,

Rough repetition roar'd in rudeſt rhime,
As clappers chinkle in one charming chime.

IN the *Lynn-Magazine* (which is avowedly of
DICK's compilation) he labors hard to account
for the conduct of the electors, as well as of
the candidates, and the different intereſts on
which they ſtood : but all in vain ! neither DICK's
coaxing nor *joſtling* could prevail with the freemen
to think *as he did.* The following " *liſt of the
horſes and colours of the riders, which entered for
the town plate at Lynn-Regis in Norfolk, on Monday,
March* 21, 1768 ;—*rode by gentlemen ;*" is a meta-
phorical relation of the conteſt and its iſſue.

" Mr. *Walpole*'s pye-bald colt, NO-BODY, *J. D—e,*
rider in black, and yellow, -   -   -   1ſt.

" Sir *John Turner*'s beautiful Highland poney,
GENERAL WARRANTS, *C. T.* rider, in black-
and-all-black, -   -   -   -   2d.

" Mr. *Molineux*'s bright bay horſe, LIBERTY,
J. F. rider, in blue and orange, -   -   diſt.

" GENERAL WARRANTS took the lead, and
" went off at three-quarter ſpeed, but pulled in
I   " upon

" upon perceiving LIBERTY lying by; and No-
" BODY appeared to be *double-diſtanced* at firſt ſtar-
" ting, having *no legs to run upon:* in the middle
" of the heat, the odds againſt No-BODY were ten
" to one, then twenty to one, and ſoon after an
" hundred to one, when, all on a ſudden, LIBERTY
" ſtopp'd running, ſuffered No-BODY to paſs by
" him, and *walked* over the courſe the remainder
" of the heat, to the great mortification of the
" whole company preſent, and the *knowing-ones*
" were completely *taken in!* GENERAL WARRANTS
" obſerving LIBERTY to give up *running*, permit-
" ted the colt to ſlip by him too; the *rider* know-
" ing his *maſter* as well as himſelf had a regard
" for No-BODY.—N. B. Many were of opinion the
" *winning* horſe owed his ſucceſs to his *rider only.*"

BEFORE we leave the *Lynn-Magazine*, we muſt
extract from it, DICK's humorous account of a
ſpeech made on the day of election by the late
Sir W——m B——ne, Knight, M. D. " Mr.
" P—dge was ſeconded by Sir W. B. whoſe *rhe-*
" *toric* was *amazing*: if the Recorder's unuſual
" eloquence ſurprized the audience, Sir W.'s
" *tranſported* them beyond all *bounds*. His *tropes*,
" his *figures*, his *metaphors*, were *birds of paſſage*,
" perfectly at his command; they *flew* and *flapped*,
" and *flapped* and *flew*, from bench to table, from
" table to bench, and ſo round the hall; now here,
" now there, that every body had them, though
" none

" none could hold them: *natural intereft,*—Liber-
" ty,—*Joe Sparks,*—now *Folkes,* now *Turner*—
" Such a tranfition! fuch volubility of *prancing*
" periods! fuch a variety of *beautiful inconfiftencies!*
" fuch a *fweet reconciliation* of *jarring* founds! (all
" true *mufic* being built on *difcord)* fuch a fwel-
" ling majefty of language, uttered from a voice
" fo *perfectly harmonious,* and from lungs fo irrefift-
" ibly ftrong, charmed his hearers to a pitch of
" *exquifite* delight, fo that not a fingle Common-
" council-man or Alderman was free from *agita-*
" *tion;* every *body* and every *part* of a body, was
" in action: *nods, winks, nofes, fingers, toes, eyes,* and
" *tongues,* were all in *fpontaneous emotion,* marking
" applaufe and admiration wonderful!" &c.

At the fame time that our hero was bufily engaged in the controverted election for Lynn-Regis,
he was equally affiduous for his friends, Sir Edward Astley and Mr. Wenman Coke; who,
in oppofition to Sir Armine Wodehouse and
Mr. De Grey, were declared candidates for the
County of *Norfolk;* and it may be truly faid,
that *he had two irons in the fire.* Sometime after
the county election, which happened on March
23, 1768, he collected the moft material papers,
in profe and verfe, publifhed during the canvas in
1767 and 8, and printed the fame in a octavo
pamphlet of 148 pages, called The Contest.

Votum,

Votum, timor, ira, voluptas,
Gaudia, difcurfus, noftri eft farrago libelli.
JUV;

Nec enim levia aut ludicra petuntur
Præmia.——
VIRG.

FOR reafons very obvious, we do not mean to
exhibit the various manœuvres and electioneering
tactic employed during this campaign of the
paper war, in which DICK MERRY-FELLOW proved
himfelf an able, zealous, experienced officer: dili-
gently obferving the motions of the enemy, taking
every advantage of ground, bringing up frefh artillery, and attacking his adverfaries in the moft vul-
nerable part—with their own weapons, GENERAL
WARRANTS! *Liberty* of the prefs! Court influence! Penfions! Places! and a catalogue of
other grievances; real and ideal!

HE ever held an opinion, that " an idle man
" is a blank in the creation," and that " the line
" of *neutrality* at elections, had been, in general,
" exploded, and laughed at by men of fenfe." To
this maxim he religioufly adhered on moft occafions, and to this caufe may we afcribe all thofe
petulencies and feuds that fo frequently over-
fhadowed his underftanding, and left him be-
wildered in difficulties and diflike,—even with the
parties he had warmly efpoufed:—but, *private*
vices, are public benefits!

PARTY-

PARTY-fpirit is a certain contagious diftèmper
which rageŝ with greater violence in England than
elfewhere : and muft not the fource of this ma-
lady, afks a writer, arife rather from the *heart*
than from the *head*; from the different operations
of our paffions, than of our reafon ?

Furorne cæcus, an rapit vis acrior,
An culpa ?

And this will always be the cafe, whilft there fub-
fifts fo powerful an *influenza*—as perfonal intereft !
What were DICK's pureft motives, his after-con-
duct will beft explain ? perhaps he wifhed to
become of more importance, and public efti-
mation, than his natural fphere of life would
admit !

" Now to the utmoft all his labors charge,
" To fhew his mighty confequence at large."

Or, perhaps, he had an eye to the *loaves and fifhes* ?
But he was that ftrange, inconfiftent hetero-
geneous, *outrèe* being, which " all men knew and
no one regarded"—longer than he was ufeful.

THE day of nomination was on Thurfday, October 8, 1767, but the day of election was not till
Wednefday, March 23, following ; in which time,
a term of fix months, the canvas was warmly
pufhed on both fides, *fecundum artem* :

" And

[118]

"And declamation roar'd, while paffion flept."

And that rebellious teazing ulcer of poetical effu-
fion, the *cacoethes fcribendi*, had taken fuch poffeffion of the minor bards, as threatened a total diffolution of rhyme and reafon!

> All human race would fain be wits,
> And millions mifs for one that hits.
>
> SWIFT.

WE have already obferved that that, political
hydra, GENERAL WARRANTS, was the butt and
inflammatory rage of party. " General Warrants
" are illegal! General Warrants are unconftitu-
" tional! General Warrants are rods of iron for
" the chaftifement of the people of England!"
fays a Norfolk freeholder; and he adds a lift of
thofe members who voted *againft*, and of thofe
who did *not* vote againft, General Warrants.

Two very humorous *Letters*, giving an account of the meeting on the nomination day, and
the fpeeches of *Hurlo-Thrumbo*, the prize-fighter,
and of *Bullet Blunder*, of Sir *John Quickfilver* and
Mr. *Quorum Porcus*, are clearly of DICK's writing.

> *Hi motus animorum, atque hæc certamina tanta*
> *Pulveris exigui jactu compofta quiefcunt.*
>
> VIRG.

But we only extract the following note:

IN-

INTELLIGENCE EXTRAORDINARY.

*Caricatura-*Hall, July 7, 1766.

" AT a public meeting this day held, the *County* of *Dere-ham* came to a final and unanimous refolution of putting in *nomination* two Candidates to reprefent the *Borough* of *Norfolk* at the next general Election, after a previous harangue in their favor, delivered with aftonifhing eloquence by the learned Recorder of *B—ry* in *Suffolk.*

" HE recommended, in the courfe of his oration, the *re-election* of the *old* members, *who were both prefent,* and dwelt with *fingular* propriety on the *great popularity* they had acquir'd by their *fteady* and *uniform fupport* of GENERAL-WARRANTS, and their inflexible oppofition to the *Repeal* of that invaluable *Magna-Charta* for *North-America*, the STAMP-ACT : he clofed all with obferving their fpirited endeavours to *extend* the Laws of EXCISE already found fo beneficial to the *trade* and *commerce* of thefe kingdoms.

" LORD CARICATURA fpoke a great deal on the occafion, but *faid nothing*, it being his lordfhip's opinion, " that a PEER ought not to *influence* the election of a " COMMONER:" His lordfhip therefore *contented* himfelf with taking down the names, and *taking off* the *faces*, of the whole company; of the latter of which he has fince formed a very *curious* collection, to be hung up in the *grand foloon* at the *Caftle* of QUEBEC.

N. B. The *County* of *Dereham* had all the honor to dine with his lordfhip this day, and the two *old* members to *kifs* his ———"

.May General Warrants North-Briton's enflave,
And O ! may they fetter each time-ferving knave !
                                                    But

But you, ye free fouls, who for liberty look,
Huzza! with loud voices for ASTLEY and COKE.

Jan. 14, 1768.

WHO firſt began to puff and crack and boaſt
From *Yarmouth, Wells,*--and down along the Coaſt?
HOLKHAM's *rich heir?* or *ſweet* Sir ARM—E, ſay?
Imperious AST—Y? or the *meek* DE-G—Y,
Whoſe gentle carriage ſteals all hearts away.

" ILLEGAL and not warranted by Law, "
Who from theſe Words could different Meanings draw?
HOLKMAN's *rich heir?* or *ſweet* Sir-ARM—E, ſay?
Imperious AST—Y? or the *meek* DE-G—Y,
Whoſe gentle carriage ſteals all hearts a way?

AMONG the fugitive pieces, here ſelected from
DICK's publication of the *Conteſt,* none was more
openly avowed than the following Song; which,
for ridicule and pointed ſatire, is equal to any
produced on the occaſion : and if we may judge
of their feelings by the ſeverity of the lampoon,
this line, from the *Bath guide,* is not inapplicable
from the parties to the author.

You come like an impudent wretch, to attack us !

Or, in the words of *Juvenile,*

————*Monſtrum nullâ virtute redemptum
A vitüs.* — — —

SONG.

SONG, wrote by R-CH--D G-RD-N-R, Efq.

R--NH-M IN THE DUMPS; or, a *Quo War-
ranto* againft the conftitution.

Tune, " The Archbifhop of Canterbury."

I.

ONE morning early, Sir ARM—E went
    To R--NH-M in great forrow;
Some folks relate 'twas with intent
    To bid the *peer* good morrow;
When at the door a *tall boy* ftood,
    All drefs'd in buff and black, Sir!
Who ftop'd him fhort, and faid, " *Sir Knight,*
    " As you came you may go back, Sir!"
                        Fol de rol lol, &c.

II.

" I know thee well, the *Knight* reply'd,
    " A *Colonel*—fo am I, Sir!
" And with your leave, good Colonel *Bluff,*
    " I muft, and will pafs by, Sir!"
" O! no, O! no! the *Colonel* he faid,
    " Tho' I am the *great* DE-G—Y, Sir!
" My *Lord* fees none but pimps and fools,
    " And *J-mmy J-n-s,* to day, Sir!"

III.

While thus the heroes parlying ftood,
    Flew ope' a door, and lo! Sir!
The firft came *J-mmy J-n-s,* and next,
    The pimps all in a row, Sir!

My

My *Lord* he bow'd, my *Lord* he fcrap'd,
    My *Lord* he pull'd his cheek, Sir !
And twirling his neck and head about,
    He thus vouchfafed to fpeak, Sir !

IV.

" O woe is me ! alack ! a day !
    " Poor *Ch-rly* * is no more, Sir !
" And I, alas ! am no body now,
    " Who was but little before, Sir !
" Sir ARM—E you, and you DE G—Y,
    " And on you, *J-mmy J-n-s*, I call, Sir !
" O ! weep with me, O ! weep—for why
    " Lord B—CK—NGH—M fees me fall, Sir !

V.

" What ! tho' I'm fcamp'ring over fea,
    " Chief Conftable to the K—g, Sir !
" My ears will morning, noon, and night,
    " With C—KE and ASTL—Y ring, Sir !
" I'm cut to the brain, ftand off ! ftand off !
    " For I am mad outright, Sir !
" Of GENERAL WARRANTS I think all day,
    " And I dream of Lord B—TE all night, Sir !

VI.

" Much injur'd fhade of L—IC—ST—R fee !
    " Thy full revenge is taken,
" From *Luttrell* and from *Alb-marle*
    " I fcarcely faved *my Bacon* ;

---

* Surely our Hero does not mean *Ch-rly Stu-rt ?* if he does
he deferves a ———

" And

" And now Sir EDW—RD, gallant Knight,
" Is hitting me hard knocks, Sir !
" O what the Devil had I to do
" With Sir EDW—RD and his Fox, Sir?

VII.

" Come, Juftice R-ſh, come aid me now,
·" His fury for to check, Sir !
" Bring all our ſons of terror down,
" O ! bring them from QU—B—C, Sir !
" QU—B—C ! harſh found ! it tortures me,
" W—LFE put me on the flanks, Sir !
" When M-RR-Y ftood where I ſhould have been,
" In front of all the ranks, Sir !

VIII.

" Where's B—C—N? here! where's T—RN—R?
" here !
" All right good men and true, Sir !
" Pluck out the Orange from your hats,
" And flip,in the plaid and blue, Sir !
" Norwich ſhall ftorm, and Lynn ſhall rant
" And roar for the conſtitution,
" We'll drink Lord B—TE upon our knees,
" And d-mn the revolution.

IX.

" Cheer up, my militia bully-backs !
" Look big ! and never fear 'em ;
" For what can C—KE and ASTL—Y do,
" When we have the county of Dereham?"

So

So faying, he kifs'd the W—RH—M *Knights*
Sir ARM—E and DE-G—Y, Sir !
And off they went quite happy all,
And fure to win the day, Sir !

Fol de rol lol, &c.

Nov. 4, 1767.

To the Author of the Epigram in the Norwich
Mercury of January 9, ending with the following line in favor of an old member.

" As a foldier profefs'd, goes before a recruit."

E P I G R A M.

OLD foldiers who defert their country's caufe
And fight againft its *freedom* and its *laws,*
No corps admit to take their poft again,
But young recruits become the front-rank men.

Swaffham, Jan. 9, 1768.

S O N G,

Addreffed to Sir EDW-RD ASTL-Y, and WENM-N
C-KE, Efq.

Tune—" The women all tell me I'm falfe to my lafs."

I.

YE fons of fair freedom affift a good caufe,
Defend from oppreffion, your rights and your laws ;
Thofe bleffings fo mighty, are bleffings divine,
And toaft them each night in a bumper of wine.

Thofe bleffings, &c.

II.

II.

Defpife all *Scotch* tools, who your intereft crave,
They mean nothing elfe, but yourfelves to enflave;
Then O! give your votes, at fweet liberty's fhrine,
And to AsTL-Y and C-KE fill a bumper of wine.

And to Aſtl-y and C-ke, &c.

III.

No time-ferving fycophants ever believe,
Their boafting is felfifh, they mean to deceive;
But with men of true honor all heartily join,
And wifh them fuccefs in a bumper of wine.

And wiſh them fuccefs, &c.

IV.

Remember fam'd WILKES, who to exile was fent;
Black rancor and malice both join'd the intent;
He fuffer'd for freedom; then let us combine,
And wifh him redrefs in a bumper of wine.

And wiſh him redrefs, &c.

V

May GEORGE long reign over us, peace on us fmile,
And a free trade and commerce diftinguifh our ifle;
May our fenate be juft, and in liberty fhine,
And we drink applaufe in full bumpers of wine.

And we drink applauſe, &c.

The

The following Verfe, as it relates to DICK
MERRY-FELLOW, we infert from a Song
called *Meafure for Meafure*, publifhed by the
adverfe party.

B U T when debauch'd by *merry* DICK,
    The mufe herfelf mifcarried,
We much deplor'd the naughty trick,
    For DICK you know is married :
O prithee DICK ! no longer roam
    In fearch of foreign pleafure :
With Mrs. G-RD-N-R ftay at home,
    She'll Meafure give for Meafure.

K-mb-rley G H O S T,

I.

'**T** W A S at the awful noon of night,
    When ghofts and goblins meet,
There ftood a pale and lanky fpright
    Clofe by Sir ARM—'s feet,

II.

Wak'd from his late Lethæan cup,
    The *Knight* began to ftart,
With looks aghaft,—and rifing up,
    He faintly faid—what art ?

III.

Thy *brother* comes, the phantom cries,
    Thy conduct to upbraid ;
Which muft thy living friends furprize,
    And e'en alarm the dead.

IV.

IV.

Our kindred ghofts are in amaze
  To hear this wond'rous change,
The friends of your late happier days,
  H—RE, ASTL—Y, and L'ESTR—NGE.

V.

In *nobles* O! put not your truft,
  Divide and *rule's* their aim;
Recal paft times, and know you muft,
  There is no help in them.

VI.

Think on the glorious *thirty-four*,
  When I this honor gain'd,
Againft that domineering pow'r
  Which now *you* call your friend.

VII.

Such friends that veer and tack about,
  Deceitful are I ween;
And if they could not keep *me* out,
  They ne'er can bring *you* in.

VIII.

But hark!—the cock—I've but one word,
  One parting word, to fay,
Beware of R———m's faithlefs *Lord*,
  Nor truft too far DE G—Y.

IX.

IX.

The *Knight* at firſt with horror ſhook,
And trembling every limb,
Takes t'other nap, and when he woke,
Miſtook it—for a DREAM! .

C I N D E R E T T A;

A Mock Paſtoral. *Detur Digniori.*

DOWN dropt her *bruſh*; the *diſh-cloth* thrown aſide,
And loſt was all the *kitchen*'s ſilver pride;
Scarce would the deep majeſtic *bellows* blow,
The lab'ring *jack* would hardly, hardly go;
Dull was the *braſs*, unwaſh'd her *earthen-ware*,
And *Tabby* ſlept neglected in the chair:
Love wrought the change, 'twas love that had betray'd,
When thus in doleful dumps bewail'd the maid:
' Go, gentle gales! and bear my ſighs away,
' Ah! why ſo long does *Hurlo-thrumbo* ſtay?
' Why form'd dame nature woman's love ſo ſtrong,
' Or, why art thou ſo tempting and ſo long?
' Reſound my *tubs*, my hollow *tubs* reſound;
' Ah me! that love ſhould give ſo deep a wound!
' Why in that *Houſe* * ſhouldſt thou ſo ſtrive to *ſhine*,
' Is it more *clean* or better *kept* than mine?
' Alas! I'm told (but they are lies, I ween)
' That *dirty* houſe no mortal yet could *clean*:

---

* Parliament.

' *Rub*

' *Rub* as they will, and *polish* as they can,
' *Penfions* and *bribes* will iron-mould the man :
' Go, gentle gales ! and bear my fighs away!
' Ah ! why fo long does *Hurlo-thrumbo* ftay ?
' Why feeks my foldier forts or city-walls,
' When I can make, my love—lefs hurtful *balls.?*
' Why to the camp muft *Hurlo-thrumbo* fly,
' When I can raife, and you befiege—a *pye ?*
' If thou muft fight, for thou art born to wield,
' Oh ! fight—in *pafte*—the heroes of the field :
' When yefter-morn I turn'd my *jack* around,
' The *falt-box* fell portentous to the ground :
' Thrice mew'd the *Cat*, and thrice he flew on *Tray*
' Oh ! think on this, and thy election-day !
' Die, CINDERETTA ! eafe thy hateful fmart,
' Ambition's now the miftrefs of his heart:
' Ah me ! each object that thefe eyes can view,
• Brings to my mind fome pleafing form of you :
' When in this hand the *polish'd fpit* I hold,
' Thy fhape is here, for thou art *long* and *cold :*
' If I the *cleaver* take, the *joint* to part,
' Thy abfence then is cleaving of my heart :
' Or, if I ftrive the *kitchen-fire* to mend,
' Thofe eyes are flaming at the *poker's* end :
' Go, gentle gales ! and bear my fighs away !
' Ah ! why fo long does *Hurlo-thrumbo* ftay ?"
Thus wail'd fhe, tearful, to herfelf alone,
The hollow *tubs* re-echoing every groan :
When lo ! her much-lov'd hero ftood to view,
And her heart flutter'd as he nearer drew :
She fought the *garret* for her Sunday's pride,
Pinn'd on her *nims* *, and *brush'd* the *fleas* afide.

---

* Shift fleeves.

K   The

The bufy Sylphs attend the dreffing fair,
This clears the *fcurf*, and this *pork lards* her hair :.
This with its breath reduc'd her tear-fwol'n eye,
Another fans the pouting noftrils dry.
Down came the damfel with fuperior grace,
With all the *ftew-pan's* radiance in her face :
So *dredg'd*, fo finifh'd, and fo foft her look,
Now trips a goddefs, and now fmiles a *cook* :
Flies to her hero, with refiftlefs charms,
And clafps the *long*, *cold* C-L-N-L in her arms.

March, 18, 1768.

The foregoing burlefque paftoral, is wrote in
an eafy flow of chara&teriftic, and much humor.
The following heroic is rather labored, and too
fevere ;—in fome parts unjuft : but an ele&tion-
mufe, like a good hunter, muft not ftop at any
thing, however hazardous.

The Battle of DEREHAM, or the Annual
NORFOLK-JIG *, as it was exhibited before
Lord *********.

————————*Hæ Nugæ feria ducant*
In mala.————————

. I.

N E A R *Dereham* riding t'other day,
   I faw the *troops* in proud *array*

----

* See Hogarth's print of the Times,

With

With looks fo *fierce* and big,
I was afraid they'd come to *blows*,
Till ********** bade the triple-rows
    Begin his *Norfolk-jig.*

II.

Heavens! with what tremenduous air
The *fubalterns* began to ftare!
    The *captains* led the *van:*
The *major*'s horfe was feen to prance:
The *drums* to fkip, the *fifes* to dance,
    They caper'd, jig'd, and ran!

III.

Up hill and down, o'er hedge and ditch,
Regarding neither head nor breech,
    In eager thirft of *glory:*
Truft me, not fafter could they fly—
To *battle*, were the *French* as nigh
    As *Scarning-wood* before ye.

IV.

To number, O! 'twould be in vain
How many cocks and hens were *flain!*
    Here fprawl'd a bleeding pig!
The cackling geefe before them fled,
There many a wadling duck lay dead,
    Crufh'd in the *Norfolk jig.*

V.

Three turkey-cocks in *ambuftade,*
View'd with difdain the *havoc* made,

They

They fwell'd, with hoftile ire;
They fwell'd, as thro' the bufhes green,
Their *fcarlet* gills were flaming feen,
And nigh they drew and nigher.

VI.

Appal'd at once the *martial* band
Halt at the *General*'s command,
  In wild amaze each *rank*;
The toe projeƈted 'gan to quiver,
To flutter much the heart and liver,
  And vifages grew lank.

VII.

So on that ever-glorious plain,
Where *England*'s warlike fon was flain,
  True *foldier*, great in all!
———— the conquering *troops* could check,
In full purfuit and fave $\mathcal{Q}$——*c*,
  From inftantaneous fall.

VIII.

For he obferv'd, though void of fear,
That *Bougainville* was in the rear,
  Wolfe dead! the *French* advancing!
'Twas time to fet all matters right,
He thought, and fo he ftopp'd the *fight*,
  As now he did the dancing.

IX.

The *Dereham* chiefs, the *battle* done,
With the fame fpeed and fpirits run

To

To dine, and take their *pay*;
Firſt from theit *gaiters* wipe the mud,
And from their reeking *ſwords* the *blood*,
Such ſlaughter was that day !

X.

Vain fleeting joys ! the month is paſt,
To other arts our *warriors* haſte ;
The *annual jig* is o'er ;
Thus the mock-heroes on the ſtage,
" Strut out their hour in empty rage,
" And then are heard no more."

F I N I S   C O R O N A T   O P U S.

Norwich, March 19, 1768.

Though we find the followiug very excellent
ſong among Capt. MERRY-FELLOW's collection,
we do not eſteem him as the author ; neither do we
believe it was *wrote for any electioneering* purpoſe,
nor aimed at any of the gentlemen to whom he
has thought proper to addreſs it, but is a general
ſatire on the militia——*of that day.*

Sir DILBERRY DIDDLE, Captain of Militia;

Humbly inſcribed to the Right Hon. *L. T.* Sir
A. W. Bart. and *T. De G.* Eſq. Colonels in *ordinary* of Militia.

OF all the *brave* captains that ever were ſeen,
Appointed to fight by a King or a Queen ;

By a Queen or a King appointed to fight,
Sure never a Captain was like this brave Knight.

Derry, &c.

He pull'd off his flippers and wrapper of filk,
And foaming as furious as—whifk-pated milk;
Says he to his Lady, " my Lady, I'll go—
" My company calls me, you muft not fay no."

Derry, &c.

With eyes all in tears, fays my Lady—fays fhe,
" O cruel Sir *Dilberry!* do not kill me!
For I never will leave thee, but cling round thy *middle*,
And *die* in the *arms* of Sir Dilberry Diddle." ·

Derry, &c.

Says *Diddle* again to his Lady, " My dear!
(And with a *white* handkerchief wip'd off a tear)
The *botteft* of actions will ever be *farce*,
For fure thou art *Venus!*" fays fhe, " Thou art *Mars*."

Derry, &c.

A while they ftood fimp'ring, like Mafter and Mifs,
And Cupid thought he would have given one kifs;
'Twas what fhe expected, admits no difpute,
But he touch'd his own finger, and *blew a falute*.

Derry, &c.

By a place I can't mention, not knowing its name,
At the head of his company, *Dilberry* came;
And the drums to the window call every eye,
To fee the *defence of the nation* pafs by.

Derry, &c.

Ol

Old *bible-fac'd* women, through fpectacles dim,
With hemming and coughing, cried, " Lord it is him !"
While the boys and girls, who more clearly could fee,
Cry'd, " *Yonder*'s Sir *Dilberry Diddle*—that's he !"
                                        Derry, &c.

Of all the fair ladies that came to the fhow,
Sir *Diddle's* fair Lady ftood *firft* in the row ;
" Oh, *charming*, fays fhe, how he looks *all in red !*
How he *turns out his toes*, how he *holds* up his *head !*"
                                        Derry, &c.

Do but fee his *cockade*, and behold his *dear* gun,
Which fhines like a *looking-glafs* held in the *fun* ;
O ! fee thyfelf now, thou'rt fo martially fmart,
And look *as you look'd* when you *conquer'd my heart.*
                                        Derry. &c.

The fweet-founding notes of Sir *Dilberry Diddle*,
More ravifh'd his ears, than the found of a *fiddle*,
And as it grew faint, that he heard it no more,
He foften'd the word of *command* to—*encore.*
                                        Derry, &c.

The *battle* now over, without any *blows*,
The heroes *unarm* and ftrip off their clothes ;
The *Captain* refrefh'd with a fip of *rofe-water*,
Hands his *dear* to the coach, bows, and then fteps in after.
                                        Derry, &c.

John's orders were fpecial, to drive very *flow*,
For fevers oft follow *fatigue*, we all know ;
But prudently cautious, in *Venus's lap*,
His head under *her apron*, brave *Mars* took a nap.
                                        Derry, &c.

K 4   He

He *dreamt*, fame reports, that he *cut all the throats*
Of the *French*, as they landed in *flat-bottom'd boats* :
In his *sleep* if such *dreadful destruction* he makes,
What HAVOC—ye gods! shall we have when he *wakes*.

Derry, &c.

The GHOST of KIMBER.

Tune—" Hosier's Ghost."

I.

A S at midnight, half distracted,
Poor Sir ARM—E weeping laid ;
Hurt to think how mad he acted,
And the *dupe* he had been made.

II.

All his hopes and friends declining,
All his *cash*, so idly spent ;
Loud he curst that day of joining,
When to RAIN——M first he went.

III.

Thus opprest, with thoughts so horrid,
Lo! aside the curtain flew,
When a Ghost, with low'ring forehead,
Stood presented to his view.

IV.

Brother ARM—E, thou art doing
(Said the shade) no honest part ;
Can'st thou seek thy *cousin's* ruin,
Led away by T—NSH—D's art ?

V.

V.

Know! I scorn thy hateful measures,
 And thy junction do disown ;
Has not *M lt-n* spent its treasures,
 When our *father* sav'd his own ?

VI.

What is HONOR when neglected?
 On my best of friends you frown ;
Hun-ston too you know, protected,
 And they *pull'd* Sir ROBERT *down*.

VII.

But O ! ARM—E, pray remember
 What an injur'd Ghost declares,
T—NSH—D loves not you, nor KIMBER,
 Nor would stir to save your ears.

VIII.

But farewel ! the cock is crowing,
 I must, now, no longer stay ;
Stop those tears, which now are flowing,
 For thy lost *election-day*.

IX.

For when ASTL—Y *rides victorious*,
 And the happy day be won,
You shall shrink away, inglorious,
 Unsupported, and undone !
LYNN, *Feb.* 5, 1768.

On

On Sir ARM—E's fuddenly growing *blind* and *deaf*, upon hearing the voice of *Truth*,

THE *voice* of *Truth*, of old how great,
Our anceftors declare;
Eyefight it gave unto the *blind*,
And to the *deaf* an *ear*.

In our degenerate days, alas!
A fad reverfe we find;
Thofe who could *hear* before are *deaf*;
And who could *fee* are *blind*.

NORWICH, *March* 16, 1768.

ON Wednefday March 23, 1768, the election for Knights of the fhire came on at the Caftle of Norwich, and next morning the High-Sheriff declared the ftate of the poll to be as follows :—

Sir Edward Aftley, Bt. of Melton-Conftable, 2977
Thomas De Grey, Efq. of Merton, . — 2754
Sir Armine Wodehoufe, Bt. of Kimberley, 2680
Wentham Coke, Efq. of Holkham, — 2610

and that the two former were duly returned to reprefent the County of Norfolk in parliament.

THUS were the ftrenuous exertions of *Country* and *Court* intereft brought to an iffue, and each had caufe to triumph in the choice of a member;

yet

yet the following ftate will fhew that the Country intereft was the ftrongeft *in point of numbers* :—

Votes for Sir Edward Aftley and Mr. Coke — 5587
    Sir Armine Wodehoufe and Mr. De Grey 5434
                            —————
                            153

THE old party-diftinction, *Whig* and *Tory*, was not unfuccefsfully revived, and the confiftency, or inconfiftency, of political fentiment in the feveral candidates and their adherents, was played off with the ufual climax. Rhetorical lightning flafhed from figure to trope,—from trope to figure, and the impetuofity of writers ran on in that *ti-tum-ti* infipididity which rather palls than awakens, and difgufts rather than convinces : But " pleas'd with a feather, tickled with a " ftraw," they are infenfibly lead on, whether in confequenee of feeling a *goût* or of touching a *doceur*, it matters not—fo that they divert the current of popularity into its proper channel.

THAT the liberty of the fubject is infringed by an extenfion of power, or a mifapplication of authority ? is a trite but melancholy truth, verified by daily experience ; yet thofe *in office* are blind to the evil, and deaf to the cure : And happy, themfelves, in the *fanctum fanctorum* of Majefty, they are callous to the diftreffes of others, and totally infufceptible of that general PHILANTHRO-

                                    PHY

THY which extends from the center, *self-love*, in circles to univerfallity, fo finely defcribed by Pope :

Friend, parent, neighbour, firft it will embrace,
His country next, and next all human race.

As every poifon carries with it an antidote, fo may the people remedy that very evil, *once in feven years*, of which they complain during that period ; but their infatuation is fuch, that the only ufe they make of their fhort-lived *liberty*—is, to apply an old plaifter to a frefh wound ; and, as if by fafcination, bring on themfelves that imbecillity and contempt, which the fuccefsful candidate of a certain borough had the *fincerity* to fhew his conftituents : " I bought you, and I " will fell you !" In this medium of venality and folly may we, like " Patience on a monu- " ment fmiling at Grief," remain till, according to Milton, we fee " Golden days fruitful of gol- " den deeds," or in words more to the prefent purpofe, fee " virtuous days fruitful of virtuous " deeds."

Few inftances of that honeft fpirit congenial with public faith, are to be met with. Modern patriots profefs a great deal—but mean very little ; and that regard due to their country is fwallowed up in party-feuds and corruption. Not fo the worthy

worthy Yarmouth-reprefentative in 1681 : " You
" have chofen me *freely*, and I will *ferve you* faith-
" fully."—Not fo the member for Chichefter, on
" offering his fervices again: I found you *free*,
" and fo, for any act of *mine*, you remain."

WE ought not to meafure men's intentions by
their *fuccefs*, for it is cruel, in the extreme, to condemn a legiflator, or a military commander,
merely becaufe he is over-powered by numbers.
His abilities and integrity may be brilliant tho'
his efforts may lack luftre : *the race is not to the
fwift, nor the battle to the ftrong :* but, alas! the
nation hath recently had fuch fatal- experience
of this difpofition, not only among the people,
but in adminiftration, that when our confidence
is no longer in men of merit, we ought not to be
furprifed at finding the army-lift full of adventu-
rers and defperadoes; who are not actuated by
principle, nor limited by intereft; whofe neceffities
force them into the fervice, and whofe fenfe of
honor is not fcrupuloufly high. The fervice
becomes no longer the *primum mobile* of all human
diftinction, when a *commis**, an obfcure fellow‡, or
a traitor†, is put at the head of a corps; or, when
the bold, juft, hardy veteran, muft give rank to a
petit maitre, who probably has nothing to recommend him but a tafte for *drefs*, or his being the il-

---

* F—ll—n, &c.   ‡ Mc. C—k, &c.   † One Arnold.

legitimate

legitimate of a profligate peer, or court fycophant.
The nature of the fervice at fea, fhields the navy
from being contaminated by men of this defcription; but that fhameful and iniquitous partiality
which is, on every occafion, exercifed by the ****
**** of the *********, hath driven many, very
many, able and experienced Commanders a-fhore.
From this digreffion we fhall return to our hero,
who we find difcufing electioneering politics with
that fhort-fighted perfpicuity fo well expreffed by
Mr. Burke in the Houfe of Commons: -

> When fo much fenfe and fkill go hand in hand,
> The more we read, the lefs we underftand.

This *extempore* and well-applied couplet brought
to his mind the obfervation of Horace, *fi matura
negat, facit indignatio verfum.* '

CLACKCLOSE* TRIUMPHANT.

Hic cæftus artemque repono. VIRG. Æn. 5. l. 434.

YE *Clackclofe freeholders,* fo honeft and hearty,
Whom no bribes, or threats, could e'er turn from
your party,
Now the CONTEST is over, may fing and rejoice;
See the man whom you love is your country's choice !
See the honor of *Melton* again rear her head,
And the *Knight,* at our bidding, retire to his fhed.

---

* A hundred in Norfolk.

O l

O ! C-ke ! what a triumph, hadft thou been but join'd !
Whilft I feel for our lofs, I honor your mind,
To good or ill fate, alike calmly refign'd.
·Ye heroes, inroll'd in the *goofe-pye* cantatá,
May give them plain truth for their lying fonata;
For, in fpite of their jefting on Astl-y and C-ke,
'They had found, to their coft, this alliance no joke !
Had we known but our ftrength, 'tis a matter quite
    certain,
We had quell'd both the *knight*, and the *dragon* of
    M-rt-n.
Let us then, pay due merit to thofe worthy men,
Who have felt, unprovok'd, the fcratch of their pen.
With the lord of *Stow-hall*, fee ! the village refounds,
Who feeds every day the poor——*not his hounds :*
Diftinguifh'd by fortune, by family great,
And a foul as inlarg'd as his ample eftate.
See *Rifton's* old Sire join the patriot train,
And forget for a while, difeafes and pain !
His two gallant fons the firft fummons attend,
And with vigor fupport their relation and friend ;
Ever fwift on the wing to defend and affail,
Where their own party fhrink, or the adverfe prevail.
See St-lem-n the honeft, the theme of each voice,
Who fhines, in his circle, the true *man* of *Rofs :*
To old age and want always opens his door,
The fteward himfelf of the helplefs and poor !
See good-humor'd Saff-ry, active and bold,
And ready to face them in all their ftrong hold !
Ever cheerful and willing to help thofe who need,
Where friendfhip demands, or diftrefs wants his aid.
Let a brave *half-pay officer* bring up the rear,
Who, tho' fomething to hope for, has nothing to fear ;
                      Who

Who, took up his *pen* when he laid by his sword,
And dares to speak truth, tho' his subject's a L—d;
That sword, which in youth his enemies fled,
'Tis hard, when he's old, should *scarce give him bread:*
But learning and sense must prevail at the last,
And, I hope, will reward him the wrongs that are past :
Then, neighbours, farewel—do but stedfast remain,
We'll be ready to meet them again and again.

Cambridge Chronicle,
    April 23, 1768.

Inscription for the Pedestal of the grand Obelisk
to be erected in the Public Market-place at
East-Dereham, in the County of Norfolk.

LIBERTATI REVIRESCENTI
S.
SEJANO adulatore septentrionali
Cladem Reipublicæ
Meditante
Genti Anglicanæ
Cui Maxime Infensus erat
Per Septem Annos graviter Incumbente
Regem Optimum Arroganti nimis Facilem
Fallente Ludente
Proceres Corrumpente
Amicitias Primorum Discindente
Peste nusquam non Grassante
Et O Rem miram et incredibilem !
O Facinus Inauditum !
Senatore Fortissimo
Qui Leges Patriæ Labefactatas

In

In Seipfo Violatas
Summa cum Animi Magnitudine
Suftentarat
In Exilium Miffo
Amandato Profcripto
In tali tantoque rerum Difcrimine

EDWARDUS ASTLEIUS,
Miles

Non a Militiæ Secretioribus Confilijs
Aut indomitis Catervis
Sed vir morum Integer fed Urbanus
Sed Strenuus
Cum Strenuorum Auxilio Tempus Egeret
Perquam Maxime

LEGATUS in Senatum venit
NORFOLCIENSIS
Confentientibus Bonorum Omnium Suffragijs
Renegante Servo tantum Pecore
Univerfo Populo Plaudente
OVANTE TRIUMPHANTE.

Superbam Hanc Columnam
In Honorem Familiæ
In Memoriam Facti
LIBERTATIS Vindices Acerrimi
Et Virtutis Publicæ Cultores incorruptiffimi
CIVES DEREAMENSES
Una Voce
Extrui Voluerunt
ANNO MDCCLXVIII.

L   Lift

Lift of Pamphlets publifhed during the Conteft.

1. A LETTER to JOHN B—XT—N, of
    Sh-dw-ll, Efq. on the Contefts rela-,
tive to the enfuing Election for the County of
Norfolk.

Per Graum populos, mediæque per elidis urbem,
Ibat ovans, divumque fibi pofcebat honorem. 1768.
                                    V I R G.

2. A LETTER from the Ifland of BARATA-
RIA, to the Author of a Letter to JOHN B-XT-N,
Efq. containing a fhort defcription of the true
characters of *Sancho,* the chief-governor*; *Caledon,*
the principal fecretary †, Colonel *Promife,* Lieu-
tenant-governor‡, Sancho's jefter, and fpeaker
of the ifland; Serjeant *Ruffin,* the prime ferjeant
of the pleaders.

By RODERIGO, State-Phyfician.

Cum fint
Quales ex humili magna ad faftigia rerum
Extollit, quoties voluit fortuna jocari.
                                    J U V.

N. B. This letter was wrote and printed in
Dublin, by the gentlemen of the committee for

---

* Lord V. T——d. † Lord F—c C——ll. ‡ Right
Honble. J—n P—by.

conducting.

conducting the prefs, and, with three other letters
of the fame fize, were publifhed in the paper
called the *Public Regifter*, or the *Freeman's Journal*,
at Dublin.

Dublin Epigram on the Irifh Addrefs upon the late Peace.

" QUOTH Teague to Paddy, in a tone outrageous,
" The devil burn their houfes—advantageous !"
Paddy, more cool : " They know in England, brother,
" We Irifh *fpake* one thing, and *mane* another."

---

3. A LETTER to the Author of a letter to JOHN B-XT-N, Efq.

*Non equidem hoc ftudeo, bullatis ut mihi nugis
Pagina turgefcat, dare pondus idonea fumo.*

PERS.

4. REMARKS on the LETTER to JOHN B—XT—N, Efq.

*Falfus honor juvat et mendax infamia terret
Quem? nifi mendofum et mendacem ? ——*

HOR.

On foreign mountains may the fun refine
The grape's foft juice, and mellow it to wine,
With citron groves adorn a diftant foil,
And the fat olive fwell with floods of oil :
We envy not the warmer clime that lies
In ten degrees of more indulgent fkies :

'Tis

'Tis liberty that crowns Britannia's iſle,
And makes her barren rocks, and her bleak mountains
    ſmile,
         Addiſon's Epiſtle to Lord Hallifax.

5. A LETTER to the Author of a Letter to
Mr. B—XT—N, in which it is proved, that
the deſign of that letter has been entirely miſ-
underſtood, and that the author of it is the real
friend of Sir EDW—RD ASTL—Y and Mr.
C—KE.

Aut laudi ſimulatione detrahere aut vituperationi laude.

                             QUINT.

6. TWO LETTERS from a Citizen of Norwich, giving an account of a pariſh meeting
held October 8, 1767, for the choice of officers for the year enſuing: alſo of the ſpeeches
of *Hurlo-Thrumbo*, the Prize-fighter and Church-
warden, and of *Bullet-Blunder*, the Steward of the
manor, and deputy Writing-maſter; with other
curious anecdotes.

              By Mr. NO GHOST.

Hi motus animorum atque hæc certamina tanta,
Pulveris exigui jactu compoſta quieſcunt.   V I R.

7. The HONEST ELECTOR's Propoſal for
rendering the votes of all conſtituents throughout
the kingdom, free and independent.

              By C. W.

Ne, pueri, ne tanta animis aſſueſcite bella;
Neu patriæ validas in viſcera vertite vires!   V I R G.

                                8. The

8. The COUNCIL.

9. The BATTLE of DEREHAM; or, The ANNUAL NORFOLK JIG; as it was exhibited before *M——r G——l* Lord Vifcount ✱✱✱✱✱✱✱✱.

Hæ nugæ feria ducunt

In mala ——–

10. The CONTEST; or a collection of the moft material papers, in profe and verfe, publifhed during the controverted election for the county of Norfolk in 1768. Containing, amongft other things, reafons for not voting for Sir E. A. and Mr. C. publifhed the Saturday before the election, with *contre* reafons for doing it, not before publifhed; a fhort account of the tranf-actions on the day of election, with a general view of the poll, and ftrictures on the admired fpeeches of Sir W. B—ne, and T. G—ne, Efq. interfperfed with fome anecdotes of a noble L——, taken from the remarks, &c.

The following fong is the only piece which Dick is faid to have wrote on the contefted election for the city of Norwich, which came on, Saturday, March 18, 1768.

Old

OLD NIC on a SECOND VISIT to NORWICH.

A NEW SONG.

Tune, " The Archbifhop of Canterbury."

O LD NIC put out of his road one day,
   By ill-defigning people,
Flew up to fee where abouts he was,
   And perch'd on NORWICH *fteeple* :
The D—n who was at St. *Andrew's* hall,
   In Gr-nv-lle's fcarfe and gown, Sir !
By chance efpied him light and afk'd,
   If he would not venture down, Sir !
          Fol derol lol, &c.

Swift as an arrow from a bow,
   He fhot upon the ground, Sir !
The D—n he took him by the hand,
   And turn'd him round and round, Sir !
Ah ! Mr. *Satan !* time I find
   The devil himfelf will alter ;
For, like my *predeceffor,* Sir !
   I took you for Doctor S—lt—r.
          Fol derol, &c.

Time, Mr. D——n, the *Devil* replied,
   Our *optic* nerves will weaken,
For 'twas but t'other day I vow,
   I pafs'd for the A——h-D-c-n :
For that *white-liver'd* p——p and p——ft,
   Believe me, I was taken,
As from a *midnight* rout I ftole,
   And fupping with NED B-C-N.
          Fol derol, &c.

The

The Pope of *St. Giles's* juft was come,
From giving *extreme unction*,
He prefs'd me hard to go to *Hunn's*,
And *fpirit* up a *JUNCTION*:
O! no, faid I, in plots I choofe
A *Proteftant* divine, Sir!
My *very good friend* the D——n is there,
And he knows 'tis a *trick* of MINE, Sir!

Fol derol, &c.

The D—— he moft obfequious bow'd,
And cried, " My Lord the *Devil!*
" Arch-D——'s and D——'s can do no good,
" Yet one way cures the evil:
" Do, BEEVOR, take *along* with *you*,
" I'm fure, I'm not miftaken:
" O! no! quoth the Devil, if *that's the cue*,
" I'll *fly away* with B——N."

Fol derol, &c.

March 1, 1768.

AFTER the buftle and convulfed ftate of men's minds, when that univerfal chaos and confufion, into which a contefted election naturally involves us, hath returned to order, and that the poetic furor is almoft exhaufted by extraordinary exertion, we muft not wonder, that, like two armies, debilitated by death and difeafe, who reciprocally enjoy a ceffation, nothing of DICK MERRY-FELLOW's excentric labors appear till 1778,—a lapfe of ten whole years.

L 4   HAVING

HAVING fo warmly embraced the intereft of
Sir Edward Aftley and Mr. Wenman Coke in
1758, againft the prevailing *Tory* intereft of the
Court, he feH a victim to minifterial influence;
and having in vain folicited that preferment and
promotion which military men claim as a *right*,
according to the idea of the army, after paft
fervices, abroad, and in an enemy's country,
he at length retired " far from the din of war,
" the rage of party, and the fury of religious
" faction," having firft (in 1773) been appointed
Captain in the 16th, or Queen's regiment of
Light Dragoons, to which commiffion, by the
King's letter and *fign manual*, the rank of MAJOR
by Brevet was ordered to be annexed, as to all
Captains of a certain ftanding on their re-appoint-
ment to the army from half-pay: this commiffion he enjoyed but a fhort time, when with
much difficulty, and as a great favor, he was
allowed the value of his half-pay, not equal
to his company of marines, previous to his
raifing the company of foot, as mentioned in
page 74, on the breaking out of the Spanifh
war in 1761.

" IN aggravation", fays Major MERRY-FELLOW,
" to thofe difappointments, I had the additional
" mortification of finding myfelf neglected and
" treated with bafe and deep ingratitude by thofe
" very families to whom I had facrificed my own
" intereft

"Intereſt, and that ambition which is the *life*
"*of a ſoldier*:—a ſtriking leſſon to all others,"
continues the Major, "hereafter, not to be
"too buſy in affairs of party, where, under
"a ſpecious and pretended love of their country,
"public-ſpirit, and conſtitutional LIBERTY,
"deſigning men advance their *private* ends,
"totally regardleſs of their ſupporters, whom
"they cheriſh warmly till their views are an-
"ſwered, and then abandon with the cooleſt
"and moſt unembarraſſed indifference; for, as
"Dean *Swift* truly obſerves, ' party is the
"madneſs of many for the benefit of the few."

WE heartily ſubſcribe to DICK's reflections
on the too frequent ingratitude of thoſe who,
having reached the ſummit of their ambitious
deſires, ſpurn with contempt and indifference
the friend who has ſhewn more zeal than prudence in their behalf;—but it is the way of
the world:

Virtutem incolumem odimus,
Sublatum ex oculis quærimus invidi.

WE do not, however, think that our hero had
much reaſon to complain on this head; for, if
thoſe, who, in gratitude, and reſpect to his abilities and character, wiſhed to do him ſervice,
had not been treated by him in a *hauteur* way,
they

they had fulfilled their intentions to the utmoſt*; but it was his misfortune, through life, always to ſet too high a value on thoſe petite ſervices he had rendered; and after exacting demands of a nature inadmiſſible, he would palliate an improper ſtep at the expence of his own veracity, *i. e.* independant and *diſintereſted* principles! and the peace of families.—Like the prodigal, whoſe paſſion for gaming will induce him to ſtake his whole worth upon a card at *vignt une*, or upon a *ſingle* throw of the dice! Dick would hazard a *coup de main.*

    " But man, who knows no good unmix'd and pure,
    " Oft finds a *poiſon* where he ſought a *cure.*

In 1774, the parliament was unexpectedly diſſolved, and Mr. De Grey declining a threatened conteſt, Mr. Wenman Coke was elected one of the knights of the ſhire, along with Sir Edward Aſtley, without oppoſition, but dying at London, April 1776, while attending his duty in Parliament, his ſon and heir, Thomas William Coke, Eſq. was unanimouſly returned in room of his deceaſed father, on Wedneſday, May 8. On this occaſion, a gentleman, *high* in office, delivered the following ſpeech, which, we are well aſſured, was wrote by Dick Merry-fellow.

---

* He acknowledges having received a handſome gratuity from the candidates he eſpouſed.

                                " Gentlemen,

[155]

"Gentlemen,

"The melancholy event that calls you together this day, is too well known to you all. You are met to confider of a proper perfon to reprefent this great commercial county in parliament; an object at all times important in itfelf, but rendered more fo by the critical fituation of public affairs at this juncture: it is now we want the abilities, the integrity, the unbiaffed firmnefs of the late Mr. Coke, to protect the interefts of the people: it is now we begin to feel the value of the faithful guardian we have loft!

"Your choice this day, I make no doubt, will fall upon fome gentleman diftinguifhed by a large property in Norfolk, whofe fortunes render him independent, whofe inclination is to be fo, and whofe ambition will lead him to imitate that conduct in parliament which does honor to the memory of his predeceffor, and who may fucceed the late Mr. Coke in public virtue, as well as public ftation."

AFTER having triffled away about fifty years of his life, amongft fky-rockets and paper-lanthorns, DICK MERRY-FELLOW began to think of the *utile dulci*; and having purchafed, at a very reafonable price, a neat houfe, elegantly furnifhed, and a fmall piece of land in the parifh

of

of Ingoldifthorpe and county of Norfolk, he retired thither from all military and political employments, refolving within himfelf to avoid the
extremes of foaring too high or finking too low,
having in the words of 'Virgil,—*Janique bifrontes
imago*, regulated his future conduct by the paft.

In two-fac'd JANUS we this moral find;
While we look forward, we fhould look behind.

THIS houfe, which he called *Mount-Amelia*,
in honor of the Princefs of that name, is moft
delightfully fituated on the brink of a hill which
rifes from the marfhes that fkirt the coaft,
at ten miles diftance from the port and borough
of Lynn-Regis, commanding an extenfive profpect of the channel leading to that town, on
which all fhips and veffels paffing to and fro, are
eafily diftinguifhed. It was built in the year 1745,
by the late John Davy, Efq. and ftands, as it were,
at the head of a large and fpacious bay, with the
fea in front, at the diftance of about three miles,
and which, viewed from the fea, has much the
appearance of what the French call a *cul de fac*,
in all their American iflands,

NOT far from this, at Caftle-rifing, Fœlix, a
Burgundian prieft, and the firft Chriftian Bifhop
in England, landed about 625; and Huftanfton-
Cliff, a few miles northward, is famous for being
the place where Edmund the Dane landed, who
afterwards became King of the Eaft-Angles,

Anno

Anno Dni. 857. The princely feat of that great *Whig* minifter, Sir Robert Walpole, at Houghton, is but five miles from *Mount-Amelia.* In the vicinity of that hofpitable roof, which had fo often and fo liberally fheltered the family of the MERRY-FELLOW's, we are not at a lofs to account for DICK's frequent vifits there, and the more efpecially, as well knowing that the noble lords of O—d have been great and munificent benefactors to his neceffities, from his moft primitive ftate to the moment of his diffolution; and this even when he was calling heaven and earth together in oppofition to their natural interefts in the county, and in the borough of Lynn-Regis: but, *quod liceat inter nos decere,* he conceived a *natural right* to their protection, under the moft inimical circumftances whatfoever. Content to

—— " Rove the paths of blifs, fecure
" Of total death, and carelefs of hereafter."

he could not be brought to obferve the vulgar maxim, " *that the willing horfe fhould not be too* " *hard ridden.*"

HERE, as we before hinted, did DICK promife himfelf the enjoyment of declining life, amidft the felicities of domeftic retirement and a few friends, and of remaining a mere fpectator and auditor of the great *farce* of the world, yet

fuch

fuch' is the inftability of human nature, that,
before one plan is put in execution, another
crowds upon us.

> And like the bafelefs fabric of a vifion
> Leaves not a wreck behind it.——

SHAKESPEARE.

WITH a rifing family of two fons and one
daughter, without any certain income to fupport
and provide for his children, embarraffed in his
affairs, and burthenfome to his friends, and Mrs.
G—'s relations, he conceived an idea of offering
his fervices to T. W. C-ke, Efq. of H-lkh-m,
in the capacity of AUDITOR-GENERAL, as he
termed it, to which, after many preffing folici-
tations, Mr. C-ke yielded; and that, as much
in regard to the opinion the late Mr. C-ke had of
DICK's electioneering *fervices*, as a defire of rewarding them, by placing him in an office, rather nominal than active, in which he might
probably be ufeful; but no fooner was our
hero in poffeffion of the appointment, under Mr.
C-ke's hand and feal, dated Auguft 1, 1776,
than he gave a loofe to his innate thirft of dominion, and under the authority of *Auditor-general
over all Mr. C-ke's eftates in Norfolk*, affumed the
character and dignity of DICTATOR-GENERAL.

INNO-

INNOVATIONS were propofed in the houfehold; tenants were threatened with raifed-rents, or expulfion; the truftee of Lord L—r's will awed; farms new formed; novel arrangements, under the fanction of œconomy, were to be adopted; the ftate and pleafures of genteel life reftricted to the moft rig̃d rules of *plain-failing*, and a new fet of vifitors to H-lkh-m H-ll—*of the Auditor-general's choofing* : nay, Mr. C-ke's kindred, friends, and intimate acquaintance, were to be prefcribed - - - - - on pain of difpleafure, and the reprefentative of the county of Norfolk, with ten thoufand a year in this, and almoft as much in other counties, was to dwindle into an obfcure country 'Squire, with a joint and dumpling every day, and a bottle of port to treat the parfon with on Sundays : and all this to be done *according to act of fancy, in pericranium affembled!*

REFORMATION is at all times, and in all ftates, defirable, but take care, that the remedy be not *worfe* than the difeafe. Had the *Auditor-general* been lefs officious, or accompanied his advice by plain and rational demonftration, fubmitted with refpect, and cooly confidered, it is probable Mr. MERRY-FELLOW might have enjoyed the *finecure*, as intended, during life ; but, unfortunately for himfelf, he thought Mr. C-ke's youth and inexperience would correfpond with Shakefpeare's dupe of fortune.

Who

Who will as tenderly be led by the nofe
As affes are.————

But Mr. C—ke found him' fo incorrigible,
that he was under the difagreeable neceffity of
difmiffing him, with a gratuity of two hundred
pounds, in February 1777 : this abrupt difmiffion
Dick took in fo much dudgeon, that he never
afterwards forgave it.

In March 1778, he publifhed *A Letter to Sir
Harbord Harbord, Bart.* who, he had prepoffeffed
himfelf, was the advifer of Mr. C-ke's conduct
on this occafion. This letter, which is printed
on 93 pages, octavo, 1s. 6d. is fo enveloped in
invective as to render the *denoüement* rather
myfterious. After reciting the engagement with,
and difmiffion from, H-lkh-m, with the feveral
letters, *in confidence,* that paffed between him and
Mr. C-ke, he proceeds to charge Sir H. H.
with being the fole caufe of his depofal. from
the *honorable office of Auditor-general,* by letter,
dated March 5, 1777, in which he recapitulates
his appointment, fchemes of improvement, want
of oftenfibility at the audit, *and coup de maitre* by
Mr. C-ke, in terms of great mortification. Speaking of himfelf, " he had a barren fceptre placed
" in his hands by Mr. C-ke, which commanded
" no authority, and a power in his pocket which
" challenged no refpect, fo that he faw plainly
" he was only made a tool of, and was looking
" over

" over farms, making calculations, and forming
" plans for the improvement of Mr. C-ke's
" eftates, for Sir *H-rb-rd's* furveyors and artificers
" to reap the benefit of :" Again he fays, " I will
" take upon me to fay, without vanity, for I can
" prove it, that I know more of the H-lkh-m
" eftate, and the true value and condition of
" it, than any other man in the county, and
" can do Mr. C-ke more effectual fervices."

" 'Tis a ftrange fatality attending me," continues Dick, " that after having ferved fo many
" gentlemen in this county in their interefts oc-
" cafionally, and having received no *very* particu-
" lar favors from any of them, that no fooner
" does any occurrence take place, that may pro-
" mife advantage or credit to the fmall abilities
" I poffefs, or the anxious zeal I exert, but mif-
" conftructions and mifreprefentations crowd in
" upon me ; though at the fame time fortified
" with the friendfhip and good-will of many of
" the firft people of the county."

To this private letter to Sir *H-rb-rd* from Mr.
Merry-fellow, he received an explicit anfwer,
dated March 11, 1777, difavowing any interfe-
rence with Mr. C-ke, to Dick's prejudice, at
the fame time freely conveying the fentiments of
Mr. C-ke's friends, and indeed of the whole
county, on the impropriety of vefting fo extra-

M   ordinary

ordinary a power in his hands : " that you have
" fteadily and uniformly endeavoured to ferve
" Mr. C-ke and his father, I have not the leaft
" doubt, and as far as my knowledge goes, I
" am ready to bear teftimony of, and I freely
" declare, that I wifh Mr. C-ke to give proofs
" of his kindnefs towards you, but from my fin-
" cere regard for him, cannot help being con-
" cerned that he fhould do it in a way to *give*
" *offence*, or difguft any of his friends." This
candid, and we may add, friendly reply, fo far
from removing our hero's fufpicions, only ferved
to aggravate his difappointment, which he refents
in the moft virulent terms his immagination could
devife, as the motto to the printed letter bears
fufficient teftimony.

> ———— *Abfentem qui rodit Amicum,*
> *Qui non defendit alio culpante* ————
> *Hic* NIGER eft ; *hunc tu,* ROMANE, *caveto !*
>
> H O R.

Affaffin-like, who *lurks* and ftabs his friend,
A *vile affaffin !* where he fhould defend ;
Tho' fools and *Shylock* of his virtues tell,
Avoid him, ROMAN !—He's as *black* as H—.

He that is not for me is againft me? faith holy
writ, was an invariable maxim with DICK, nor
could the moft folemn affurance of *neutrality*
fatisfy him on any point : no wonder then that
he

he perfifted to his laft moments in promulgating innuendoes and bafe calumny againft thofe who were barely negatives. With thefe inflammatory compofitions, our hero feems to threaten vengeance; " you may accidentally flide into fome " humorous fong fhould you offend a man of " poetical abilities,—*genus irritabile vatum.*"

> " Some humorous pages that perhaps might gall
> " A *fimple Simkin* B—r—d at S— ?"

And he has the *hardieffe* to talk of retaliation, as mathematicians fay, *in duplicata vel triplicata ratione.*

> Know there are rhymes, which (frefh and frefh apply'd)
> Will cure the arrant'ft puppy of his pride.
>
> P o p e.

" Have not the greateft men and greateft wits " of all ages trafficked occafionally in fatire and " ridicule, odes and epigrams, and often too " in *private* cenfure and reproach !"

He had flattered himfelf, *in golden dreams of ftate,* with an emolument of 600*l.* a year, *ex officia*; and we confefs, that he had every apparent reafon to confider himfelf as bountifully fupplied *for life.* In his letter of July 3, 1777, to Mr. C-ke, he fays, " If you do not mean, Sir, " to perfevere in your appointment of me as Au- " ditor, *at leaft for fome time,* you, have done

M 2

" me

[164]

" me the moſt *irreparable* injury:" To this he adds
ſome cavalier demands of explanation and *eclair-*
ciſſement, and concludes, that " I may retire in
" ſuch a manner as to do *honor* to *yourſelf* and
" *me*, and that you may at leaſt leave me, *where*
" *you found me.*" To this letter ſucceeded an in-
terview with Mr. C-ke, at which Mr. MERRY-
FELLOW expreſſed himſelf fully ſatisfied with Sir
H-rb-rd's declaring, *upon his honor*, he was not
amenable to the charge alledged againſt him on
the part of our hero, with which he declared
himſelf ſatisfied, *upon his honor*† ; but the following letter blew up the latent ſparks of malevolence to a furor which never after ceaſed
blazing !

To R-CH-RD G-RD-N-R, Eſq. *Mount-Amelia.*

" Sir,

" IT is with very great concern, that I find
" myſelf obliged to write to you on ſuch a ſub-
" ject; but after the very inconſiderate ſtep you
" took at Norwich in regard to my friend,
" Sir H-rb-rd, ſubſequent to the explanation
" we had on this affair at H-lkh-m, with which
" you ſeemed ſo well ſatisfied, you cannot be
" ſurprized that I think it incumbent on me to

---

† Shakeſpeare ſays, " *if a man ſwears by that he hath not,*
then is he not forſworn."

" decline

" decline receiving you any more into my
" houfe, and demanding back the appointment
" of Auditor-General, which I defire you will
" return by the bearer.

   " From, Sir,

      " Your moft obedient humble fervant,

         " TH-M-S W-LL-M C-KE."

H-LLH-M,
Auguſt 6, 1777.

   To a man of DICK's high metal, this letter
was a greater fhock than that given by the
Electrical Eel, or *Gymnotus Electricus*, or, even at
Dr. Graham's temple of celeftial brilliancy. His
anfwer (Auguft 23) to it is expreffive of his
feelings, but is a dull reiteration of tranfactions,
couched in the moft reproachful terms. " You
" muft excufe me, Sir, in *not returning* your ap-
" pointment, though I *will never act* under it."
" I confidered your appointment of Auditor of
" your eftates in Norfolk, as to continue for *life*,
" as a reward for paft fervices, as a recompence
" for *loft promotion in the army*, or, at my years, I
" fhould not have undertaken it, I affure you."

   Ad populum provoco, was the celebrated appeal
of the Romans, in all cafes of injury and injuftice,
and according to the adage, *private injuries require public redrefs*, DICK fubmitted a circumftan-
tial detail to the public eye. Whether it was

       M 3   ftrictly

ftrictly " a true one, not exaggerated or inflam-
" med," and that feveral damning proofs of ingratitude and ungenerous treatment were fuppreffed, we will not take upon us to determine ; but
this we may venture to hazard an opinion upon,
*that he had no juft grounds of complaint againft Sir
H-rb-rd H-rb-rd* ; but, every one who had any
fort of acquaintance at H-lkh-m *muft* be dragged
in to form the groupe, as the back ground or
foiledge of the picture he intended to exhibit;
pro bona publico. *Simple Simkin* or *'Squire Shallow* ;
Mr. C—ll ; the *cream-coloured* Recorder of ****;
the Derbyfhire *block-fplitter*, or the *carpenter ;* and
Old *Æthiops*, the *drogon* of G-nt-n, or *Shylock*,
have each their ratio of confpicuity.

" And every child hates *Shylock*, though his foul
" Still fits at fquat, and peeps not from its hole."

BESIDES what appears in this *public* letter of
DICK's§, many other manœuvres were made ufe
of to draw Mr. C—ke into terms of arbitration,
but our hero's demands were fo exorbitant and
prefcribed, that no gentleman could be found
willing to undertake an accommodation without
a *difcretionary* power.

---

§ A *fecond* and *third* edition made their way through the
prefs ; in one of which, he ftiles himfelf, " late Auditor-
General of the Holkham Eftates" in the county of Norfolk.

FROM

FROM the 21ſt of March till the 2d of May, Mr. MERRY-FELLOW triumphed in the rapid ſale of his letter, and the total ſilence of the H-lk-h-m *cabinet*, as he termed the particular friends of Mr. C-ke, when the following addreſs was publiſhed in the *Norfolk Chronicle*, and *Norwich Mercury*, of May 2, 1778.

" To the PUBLIC.

" HAVING waited to ſee the utmoſt efforts " of Mr. G-rd-n-r's Malice, and abilities for " abuſe; at length I think it incumbent on me " to aſſure the public, that all his *aſſertions* of " Sir H-rb-rd H-rb-rd's having done him diſ- " ſervice with me, are abſolutely FALSE——and " that all the diſcountenance I ſhew'd him " during his continuance in my ſervice, and my " final diſmiſſion of him from that ſervice, " aroſe entirely without *the advice, ſuggeſtion, or* " *even knowledge of Sir H-rb-rd H-rb-rd, or any* " *other of the gentlemen to whom it is imputed in* " *his pamphlet.*—That his conduct, whilſt in my " ſervice, being diſapproved by me; I there- " fore exerciſed that right, which, I apprehend, " every gentleman has, and diſmiſſed him with " a gratuity of two hundred pounds—which he " has not taken the leaſt notice of in his publi- " cation. The public buſtle he made at Nor- " wich in relation to Sir H-rb-rd H-rb-rd, after

" the

" the *affurances* I had given, that Sir H-rb-rd
" H rb-rd had never done him *any differvice with*
" *me*, I confidered as implying his difbelief of my
" affurances, and confequently, as fuoh, an affront
" to myfelf, that I thought it neceffary to for-
" bid him my houfe. Some time afterwards,
" finding he did not think the gratuity ade-
" quate to his fervices, I propofed to refer the
" point to arbitration, which he at firft refufed,
" though I am informed he has fince inclined to
" ——but as he has now, by his CALUMNIES
" and FALSEHOODS, forfeited every claim to
" my favor, I fhall leave him to try what the
" law will further give him.

TH-M-S W-LL—M C-KE,

H-lkb-m, April 26, 1778."

THIS *Jeu d'Efprit*, as DICK affects to confider
it, he read on Sunday the 3d, and although in
great extremity of pain by the gout in both hands,
both elbows, and both feet, he next morning
dictated the following anfwer, which was tranf-
mitted by poft to Norwich, to be inferted in the
news-papers of Saturday the 9th.

" LABORING under a fevere attack of
" the gout, I muft entreat the public to fufpend
" their opinion of the advertifement in laft Sa-
" turday's Norwich papers, fubfcribed Thomas-
" William

" William C-ke; to which a full anfwer fhall be
" given, as foon as I am in health,

" I HEREBY call on Mr. T—— W—— C-ke,
" to point out one fingle Calumny or Falfehood
" in my letter to Sir H-rb-rd H-rb-rd, through-
" out.

" His declarations relative to Sir H-rb-rd, are
" no more than Sir H-rb-rd's own declarations
" in his letter to me; which were not the fubjeƈt
" of the conteft at the affizes :—It was the other
" part of Sir H-rb-rd's letter to me that called
" for an explanation from him, and for which I
" *called him out*; and whether I believed Mr.
" C-ke or him, in their affertions, was out of the
" queftion—I wanted an explanation to a paffage
" in his letter to me, which I had a right to de-
" mand as a gentleman, and *ftill have*.

" THE 200l. draft advanced by Mr. C-ke, and
" and the 100l. draft advanced by me, were not
" *omitted* in my letter to Sir H-rb-rd, but *fup-*
" *preffed*; they were printed by themfelves in a
" poftfcript to the letter, but were not publifh-
" ed, on account of the arbitration propofed on
" the part of Mr. C-ke. I was not willing (un-
" lefs obliged) to tell the world, that H-lkh-m
" H—fe was without the paltry fum of 100l. to
" pay

" pay laborers, and to carry on family expences
" —Mr. C-ke has now *obliged* me to do it.

" As to forfeiting his *favor,* which he feems
" to fet fo high a value upon, I *defpife* his favor.
" —The favor and friendfhip of any perfon,
" in the line of conduct purfued by Mr. T——
" W—— C-ke, can do honor to no man.—I
" demand *Juftice,* and not favour!

" CALUMNIES and FALSEHOODS I deteft as
" much as Mr. T—— W—— C-ke, and I dare
" him to the proof: in the mean time, and
" 'til my health returns, I thus publicly deny
" the truth of the advertifement he has put
" his name to, and hereby declare it to be totally
" and *fundamentally* falfe.

Mount-Amelia, May 4th, 1778.

R-CH-RD G-RD-N-R."

THIS anfwer, for very obvious reafons, and for
others no lefs cogent, the printers thought proper not to admit, which produced the following hand-bill, containing, alfo, the anfwer as
above.

Mount

Mount-Amelia, May 10th, 1778.

To the P U B L I C.

" WHEREAS an advertifement figned *Tho-*
" *mas-William* C-ke, appeared in the Norwich
" papers of Saturday, May 2. And whereas an
" anfwer, contradicting the fame, was fent on
" Monday, May 4th, to the Norwich papers,
" againft the Saturday following, May 9th, and
" was refufed admittance, the printers being
" threatened with profecution by the known
" agent of Sir H-rb-rd and Mr. C-ke: Major
" G-rd-n-r finds himfelf obliged to publifh his
" anfwer in a hand-bill.

" THE Major fubmits to the impartiality of
" the gentlemen of Norfolk, whether any thing
" can more ftrongly mark the badnefs of a
" caufe, than to appeal to the public by adver-
" tifement in a news-paper, and then to fhut
" the prefs againft an anfwer.

" THIS is the firft inftance ever known in
" Norfolk of an attempt to ftop

The LIBERTY of the PRESS :

" AND it is to be hoped the Freeholders of
" the County, and the Citizens of Norwich, will
" remember it at the next general election.

THIS

THIS brought on explanations from the printers, no way interefting to the public, but tending to clear .Mr. C-ke of having made any attempt to *ftop the liberty of the prefs.* About this time a paper, called, " Thoughts of a Norfolk Freeholder," was difperfed as a temporary explanation of the 200*l.* draft, mentioned in Mr. C-ke's addrefs, and on June 1, 1778, a pamphlet of 48 pages, octavo, 1*s.* was published. *A Letter to Thomas William C-ke, Efq. of H-lkham; wherein a full anfwer is given to his advertifement publifhed in the Norfolk Chronicle and Norwich Mercury, May 2,* 1768.

Sunt quibus in fatyra videar nimis acer, et ultra
Legem tendere opus - - - . - -

HOR.

There are, I fcarce can think it, but am told,
There are, to whom my fatire feems too bold :
Scarce to " Sir H-rb-rd" complaifant enough,
And fomething faid of " Simkin" much too rough.

POPE.

Si quis
Opprobrijs dignum latraverit, integer ipfe ;
Solventur rifu tabulæ, tu miffus abibis.

HOR.

In fuch a caufe the plantiff would be hifs'd,
My lords the judges laugh, and you're difmifs'd.

POPE.

THIS

THIS publication contains, in fubftance, the letters juft given, with curfory remarks, in DICK's ufual ftile of acrimony. "If I have thofe abili- "ties for *abufe*, which you *compliment* me with "the poffeffion of, I have full fcope to *indulge* "them." "To forbid me your houfe by letter!" "Receding from a folemn act and deed, under "your own hand and feal!" "The irretrievable "injury you have done me!" "The public "buftle," &c.

"Shake not your goary G-nt-n locks at me,
"You cannot fay I did it."——

IT alfo appears that on Mr. MERRY-FELLOW's fending an account, *debtor* and *creditor*, and draw- ing on Mr. C-ke for a confiderable balance, an arbitration was propofed on the part of Mr. C-ke, to which DICK pofitively diffented, but afterwards feemed inclined to. Here the matter dropt, and here we fhall only add the laft para- graph, which breaths more candor and modera- tion than the preceding pages feems to promife. "Having now analized this extraordinary adver- "tifement, [fee page 167] which I by no means "impute to you, Mr. C-ke, for you could never "have put together a piece of writing fo repre- "henfible in every part; and having given a "detail of facts as they really paffed, I fhall "fubmit to the world and to your own breaft

"to

" to make the application : I now take my leave
" of you, Sir ; and notwithftanding all hoftilities
" that have been carried on between us, and
" which you have drawn upon yourfelf, either
" with or without the advice of others, I fhall
" conclude this letter with a fincere wifh, that
" you may never feel that anxiety, which you
" have, to fo great a degree, and for fo great a
" length of time, thrown upon the mind of,

" Sir, your moft obedient fervant,

" R-ch-rd G-rd-n-r."

Mount-Amelia, June 4, 1778.

To animadvert on a fortuitous tranfaction, of
which we have merely the *ipfe dixit* of one party,
would be rendering us liable to error and mifreprefentation ; and indeed, as the matter has turned
out not *quite* fo interefting as it was at firft appre-
hended, we may fpare ourfelves the pain of writing and you the trouble of reading more than is
confiftent with the plan of this memoir. The
great Lord Bacon of *Verulam* thinks, that the true
judgment of a writer may be formed by his
epiftolary letters, EPISTOLÆ *magis in proximo et ad
vivum* NEGOTIA *folent repræfentare quam vel* ANNALES
vel VITÆ : If fo, how eafy will it be for the very
meaneft capacity to decide on the character now
before us.

OF all the abuſe and *wormwood*, as DICK uſed to term it, under which the preſs groaned, he ſeldom left us to exclaim with the author of the Bath Guide,

What a ſcurrilous author! *Does nobody know him?*

Nor did he take much pains to conceal himſelf. He had little to *loſe* and therefore little to *fear.* He wiſhed the venom to operate in the moſt virulent manner, and was not ſtingy of the dóſe. He knew his own ſuperiority, and felt more pleaſure by giving others pain than a good chriſ-tian ought. The muſty ſayings and maxims of the patriarchs he held in the ſame eſteem with King Charles's rules,—the mere cant of hy-pocriſy! *To turn one cheek when a man has ſmote you on the other* may be orthodox, but it is not literally applicable to human nature. *Paſſive obedience* and *non-reſiſtance* is now exploded, and we ſeriouſly are of opinion, that, except the funda-mental principles of religion and morality, the other regulations of life, which the complexion of the times renders neceſſary, ſhould vary with the ſyſtem of policy, learning, and diſpoſition of mens minds : in ſhort, according to the na-ture of things. * * * * * * * * * * * *

WHILE this nation hath been ſo deeply en-gaged in a ſtate of hoſtilities with the North

American

American colonies, on which various and violent opinions have been formed, we are not to wonder that Mr. MERRY-FELLOW also entertained a *few* political ideas: and although affairs of a still clofer connection had engroffed his immediate attention, and that nothing in print conveyed to the public his strictures, yet we are warranted to fay, that he was confistent in fentiment with thofe who are emphatically called PATRIOTS: and this, we prefume, will be the more readily believed, when we reflect, that he all along acted and co-operated in principle with what are termed the *Whig*, or *Revolutionists*, now in oppofition to the destructive meafures fo fatally and fo fuccefsfully purfued by the influence and obstinacy of weak, if not wicked, men in power—to the total fubverfion of every interested and political administration for the common weal!

DISCLAIMING, ourfelves, all bias of party, prejudice, or improper motive, we must do DICK the credit to fay, that he never commended the fcheme of coercion in America, but predicted, what most difpaffionate men did, that, as the war was commenced in ignorance and impolicy, it would be carried on with imbecility and difgrace, and terminate in certain ruin to the landed and commerical interests of Great Britain: how well this *fimple* prophecy is juftified by recent events, the prefent posture

of

of affairs will *more* than prove. The moft
confummate *Quidnunc* of them all could not for-
fee the confequences in fo difmal a light :—
without one friendly ally; at war with France,
Spain and Holland; and in enmity with every
other power : (for we cannot efteem the petit carcafe-butchers in Germany as friendly)
—betrayed by fome, duped by others, and
laughed at by all! our marine difputed, the
glory of the Britifh flag *tarnifhed*, our brave
hardy foldiers acquiring honor—but not victory !
our dependencies in the Eaft and Weft-Indies
tottering; Gibraltar and Minorca attacked;
the Baltic furrounded by neutral confederates;
Portugal wavering; the Barbary ftates at a high
price; America INDEPENDENT of this country,
and Ireland ****: good God! how are we
fallen ?

AMONGST thofe domeftic evils which diftrefs
and difatisfaction broods over, are, manufactures
and commerce limited, fleets of merchantmen un-
protected, infurance high, taxation grievous, and
the national-debt enormous; add to thefe, what
is ftill more oppreffive and illegal, the public
monies improvidently fquandered on places
and penfions, inefficient and unmerited, and
every idea of reformation and œconomy exploded by contractors—who, like cormorants and

N   locufts

locusts, are devouring the vitals of their country. So perilous, and so accumulated, is the cloud which now hangs over our heads, that nothing, within human comprehenfion, but the hand of providence, can prevent its burfting in all the fury and vengeance of irretrievable calamity! *(actem eft: ilicet: perifti,* fays Terence, ruin'd and undone!) which the degeneracy of the age and the nefarious conduct of our rulers juftly draws down upon us.——*He that believeth,* faith the fifth chapter of the Chronicles of the Kings of England, *let him believe ftill; and he that doubteth, let him doubt and be damn'd!*

DESERTED by his friends, and impreffed with the *forlorn* hope, our hero fat down fullen and inirritable; heartily wearied of that buftle which his reftlefs foul ever hurried him into, he confoled himfelf in ftill poffeffing the *cacæthes fcriblerius,* which he could provoke by conception, as readily as others could by the moft fevere flagellation of Pegafus. Thus favored by the mufes, we fee him toying with the Comic, in the fhape of an Epilogue.

An

An OCCASIONAL EPILOGUE

TO THE

MERRY WIVES OF WINDSOR.

Performed by the GENTLEMEN
Of the *Weſt Norfolk* Regiment at *Southwold* in *Suffolk*,

Soon after the engagement with the *French* Fleet
commanded by Count D'ORVILLIERS and his
Royal Highneſs the Duc de CHARTRES, brother to the *French* KING, July 27, 1778; and
the Honorable Auguſtus Keppel, Admiral of
the Britiſh Fleet.

Spoken by a LADY in the Character of Mrs. FORD.

Wrote by R-CH-RD G-RD-N-R, Eſq.

WELL! Poor Sir JOHN was in a piteous taking,
And had enough, good truth, of *Cuckold*-Making!
What PATAGONIAN Female could be found
To *flirt* it with a Lover——TWO YARDS ROUND?
Who could endure, who, that had mortal Eyes,
A *Ceciſbeo* of ſuch monſt'rous Size?
'Twas not well-bred to *ſouſe* him in a pool,
Yet ſerv'd to teaze my jealous-pated fool :
And, Critics, it had ſet *you* all a grinning,
To ſee Sir JOHN pop up amidſt *foul linen.*
Our *London Dames* to gallants are more tender,
For why? *Their* MACARONIES all are ſlender :
Should the dear youth ſome hideous huſband ſcare,
A *modern* BELLE could hide him in her *hair*;
Or, take him in her hand, and wrapp'd about
In his *white* handkerchief, convey him out.

N 3   The

The fcene is chang'd—*Intrigues* have loft their charms;
Now Female bofoms beat to WAR's alarms :
THE CAMPS, how brilliant with our *Britiſh Fair !*
Cockaded hats! lac'd frocks ! and braided hair !
The CHARGING SQUADRONS our delight become,
" The ear-piercing fife, the fpirit-ftirring drum !"

When bold DE RUYTER plough'd; the wat'ry main,
And YORK, of heroes, led a gallant train,
Unheeded on our coaft th' invaders ftole,
And caught our Captains—dancing* all at *Sole* † ;
But rufhing forth, and eager for the fight,
They made the *Dutchmen dance* the foll'wing night :
Repell'd th' infulting foe, whofe chiefs no more
Hoifted a *Broom*‡ to fweep the *Britiſh* fhore.

Should *Frenchmen* fudden as the *Dutch* attack,
NORFOLK's bold fons are here to drive them back :
Once more refulgent on this little ISLE,
Our ARMS fhine glorious, and our WARRIORS fmile :
Brave as their Anceftors, and full as gay——
——I wifh the *French* might catch them at our play :

---

* When the *Dutch* Fleet advanced, all the Captains of the
Engliſh Ships were at a *Ball* on Shore, but left it immediately
and went on board on the firft advice of the Enemy.

† *Southwold.*

‡ In November 1652, during the Ufurpation of *Oliver
Cromwell,* the *Dutch* Admiral, MARTIN VAN-TROMP, having
obliged the *Engliſh* FLEET under BLAKE, who was wounded,
to retire to the *Downs* and into the *Thames,* hoifted a *Broom*
on his Main-top-maft Head, " as if he had *fwept;* or would
" *fweep,* all the Englifh Shipping out of the Channel."

O !

O ! grant it, fortune ! goddefs, let me afk it⊣
I long to *cram* young *Chartres* in a bafket :
Then launch him out to fea, and let him roam,
" The Merry Wives of Windfor," waft him home !

: This great engagement happened on May 28, 1672. The *combined* fleets of *England* and *France* lay at anchor in *South-wold Bay*. The Duke of *York*, Lord High-Admiral of *England*, commanded the *Red* fquadron; the Count *D'Etrees* the *White*, and the Earl of *Sandwich* the *Blue*: the *Dutch* were commanded by *De Ruyter*, oppofed to the Duke of *York*; *Bankart* to Count *D'Etrees*; and *Van-Ghent* to the Earl of *Sandwich*. The Dutch fleet confifted of 72 fhips of the line, and 40 frigates and firefhips: the *Englifh* had 100 men of war, and the French 40.

In the Englifh fleet were 20,000 men and 4000 guns.
In the French - - - 13,000 ————2000 ——.——
In all 33,000 men and 6000 guns.

In the Dutch - - - 22,000 men and 4000 guns.

In this defperate engagement Vice-Admiral *Van-Ghent* was killed; the Earl of *Sandwich* blown-up in the *Royal James*; and the Duke of *York* was obliged to fhift his flag from his own fhip, which was difabled, and hoifted it on board the *London*. The *Englifh* were victorious ! the *Englifh* and *Dutch* fought well, but the *French* at a diftance.

ABOUT

ABOUT this time, propofals were made for publifhing a new and complete hiftory of Norfolk in weekly fix-penny numbers, by the firft three of which (delivered as a fpecimen) it evidently appeared, that our hero had a confiderable fhare in the compilation ; but, upon enquiry, we found, that he had only engaged to furnifh the editors with his obfervations in two or three of the hundreds in the vicinity of *M—t-A——a.* Many of his remarks are judicioufly pointed, but his panygeric is as fulfome as his cenfure is fevere, and he feems, upon the whole, to be little adapted to a tafk, where precifion and impartiality is neceffary. Wherever he had an opportunity of difplaying his own learning, wit, and martial employments, he never fails of introducing *fomething*, and indeed *we* are fomewhat beholden to thofe hundreds for a part of this *memoir*, and for fome excellent monumental infcriptions in our *addenda.* However valuable the affiftance of a man of letters may be to a work of fo much confequence, we are free to fay, that without a proper idea of the *bufinefs*, improved by experience, his ftrictures may operate to its difadvantage. The hiftory of a county is a very improper channel to convey fpleen or ill-nature through : private tranfactions, unlefs of exemplary merit, are fubjects too trivial for public record, and we are very happy to obferve, that a timely check was put upon Mr. MERRY-

FELLOW'S

FELLOW's attempts to revive (in that work) the controverſy between him and Mr. C-ke, in a manner indecent. and likely to be prejudicial to thoſe perſons who, at a very conſiderable ex-pence have now, 1781, completed this ardous undertaking, in ten volumes, octavo, adopting for a motto the ſaying of that humane Roman Emperor, *Imp.* N. TRAJAN CÆS. AU.

Pro me : ſi merear, in me.
For me :—if I deſerve it, againſt me.

To which we beg leave to add a motto of Lord Somers'.

Prodeſſe quàm conſpici.
Uſeful—rather than conſpicuous.

as indeed every publication of this ſerious nature ſhould be.

DICK MERRY-FELLOW now lived retired, and almoſt forgot, at *M—t-A——a*, when his eldeſt ſon, July 20, 1778, received an enſigncy in the Weſt-Norfolk regiment, commanded by the Right Honble the Earl of Orford, then lying on the coaſt of Suffolk. He, next day, had an oppor-tunity of ſignalizing himſelf, as a volunteer, with a detachment of thirty ſoldiers and thirteen ſeamen, in an engagement with a ſmuggling ſchooner off Southwold, for which, he and the other officers on that ſervice had a handſome ſilver ſword preſented to each of them, by the

com-

commanding officer, for their fpirited behaviour on the occafion. In 1779, this young gentleman was promoted to the rank of lieutenant in the faid corps, then in a *camp volant* at Aldborough in Suffolk, the place where his great grandfather, John G-rd-n-r, Efq. refided, (*See page 2.*) In 1780, he was again encamped on Tenpenny Common, near St. Ofyth in Effex, and from thence was appointed by his Majefty an Enfign in the 6th regiment of foot, cantoned at Lewis in Suffex, and in the December following promoted to a lieutenancy in a royal independent company, for which he raifed 30 men at Norwich. November 17, 1781, he received a commiffion, as Captain of a company in the 102d regiment of foot, then going to the Eaft-Indies: to this rapid promotion (being little more than nineteen years old) he fortunately fucceeded by the affiftance of a noble friend, whofe munificence and benevolent difpofition, on all occafions, is equalled only by his extenfive charity, learning, judgment, and tafte, for every polite and liberal art.

As he is defcended from parents of a military turn, we doubt not but he inherits the martial prowefs of his feveral friends. Thofe of his father we have before mentioned : by his mother's fide he was alfo in the military line, having four uncles, who ferved abroad laft war with great re-
. putation.

putation in Germany, in defcents on the coaft of
France, at Louifburg, Belleifle, Martinico, and
the Havanna, in the 5th, 69th, and 34th regiments of foot. The eldeft uncle, B-rdm-n B —m-
h—d, Efq. is now Lieutenant-Colonel of the
North-battalion of Lincolnfhire militia; the
fecond, B-nj—n B-mh—d, Efq. holds the fame
rank in the South-battalion, and the two others,
J-mes and J-hn, are Captains in the faid corps.

Occafional PROLOGUE *and* EPILOGUE *to* THE CLAN-
DESTINE MARRIAGE, *performed at the Theatre in*
LYNN-REGIS *by* GENTLEMEN, "*For the* BENE-
" FIT *of the Wives, Widows, and Families of*
" *the* IMPRESSED MEN *for* HIS MAJESTY'S SEA
" SERVICE, *belonging to the Town of* LYNN,
" *and its* ENVIRONS, *on* Monday, March 22,
" 1779."

P R O L O G U E.

Spoken by a GENTLEMAN.

AW'D to behold thefe radiant feats around,
Untrod before I trembling touch the ground ;
Train'd to no ftage, this night we humbly ftrive,
To keep for once, the Comic Mufe alive.

Compaffion gave thofe hints we here purfue,
And let Compaffion plead our caufe with you ;
We claim the feeling, not the actor's part,
Our wifh to pleafe, our aim to move the heart:

To

To eafe the mind, to ftop the trickling tear—
For this we act, for this you come to hear:
Whate'er our fate, however underftood,
We know—we feel—our motives to be good.

Far from thefe humble fcenes, by nature brave,
Our fons of Neptune mount the boift'rous wave:
For Britain's weal they nobly ftand to view,
They play their parts for us, and we for you:
Without their aid, the bleffings of our ifle
Would foon drop off, and love forget to fmile;
If, thro' their valor, we with comfort live,
Returns are claims—'tis gratitude to give—

Should here fome Critic lift his awful head
To ftrike us young new-fangled actors dead;
Ladies! from you, from you one fingle frown
Will make all well, and ftrike the monfter down:
So when fome envious cloud obftructs the day,
The fun breaks forth and pours the cheerful ray.
What heart-felt joy to fee fuch laughing eyes!—
When you are pleas'd we feel our fpirits rife:
Beauty has this peculiar art to pleafe,
You charm with rapture, and you kill with eafe;
If ought this night, your nicer ears offend,
Condemn the actor, but forgive the friend.

EPILOGUE

EPILOGUE.

Spoke by Mifs FRODSHAM, in the Character of
FANNY.

Wrote by R-CH-RD G-RD-N-R, Efq.

WHAT! GENTLEMEN turn'd Actors!—yes, 'tis
true.

And tho' to *us* it may be fomething new,
Yet noble fpirits find a road to fame,
Unknown to titles, carelefs of a name:
When public virtue warms with genuine fires,
They lay afide *Knights*, *Juftices*, and *'Squires:*
Vain is all rank that one good act debars,
Or fhrinks at any act for *Britifh tars*:
Our gallant failors, harden'd in the fight,
Will gain frefh courage from our fcenes to night;
Though far abroad, on dang'rous feas they roam,
Their honeft hearts ftill relifh thoughts of *home:*
Heave the foft figh for *little ones* behind,
Nor dream their countrymen are half fo kind.

O! what a noble conteft! glorious ftrife!
To aid the matron, helplefs child, and wife!
Thefe are *true* joys, and *lafting* pleafures yield;
For thefe, keen fportfmen quit the crowded field,
Where, breed of WATTON, fleeteft greyhounds ftrain,
O'er WESTACRE's high mound, or WEETING Plain;
Or where the wily fox, at diftance far,
Three of the QUORUM drops in WENDLING car:
Heels over head the rapid courfers turn,
And proftrate lie *three* rapid fons of BURN.

May

May heav'n preferve, if fuch diverfions pleafe,
My good Lord OGILBY from fports like thefe!
There was a lover, ladies! in good truth,
He wanted nothing—but a little *youth* :
A CORONET ! a well-bred man ! a beau !
There's fomething *aukward*—in a *gouty toe* :
My father trail'd along his new canal,
Thofe tender feet that ill endur'd the MALL.
O! had he ftrength to fcour the rifing plain,
Hills fhould oppofe, and cars obftruct in vain !

A gentle *Somerfet* is no difgrace,
Our feamen, like our 'Squires, love a *chace* :
They pitch and roll, and up they mount again,
Then hoift VICTORIOUS colours o'er the MAIN:
Or volunteers, or by fome chance impreft,
All bold alike, chace *Frenchmen* into BREST.

Let critics cavil at our play that dare,
For all who *fee* us, all are *actors* here ;
Each BEAUTY that is prefent *acts a part*,
And claims a tribute from fome grateful heart :
THEY triumph moft, and moft deferve applaufe,
Who DIE with pleafure in their COUNTRY'S CAUSE :
Whilft KEPPEL's thunders rule the vanquifh'd BAY,
MAYORS fhall addrefs, and GENTLEMEN fhall play.

———————

IN November 1779, our hero was attacked
by a very violent fit of the gout, a diforder to
which he had frequently been obliged to yield,
and to which he two years after fell a martyr.
During this fevere trial of chriftian patience, he
was feldom able to move without crutches, and
for

for more than a twelvemonth was confined to his
bed or chair; having had one of his feet laid
open feveral times with the lancet, and above
two ounces of chalk taken from it;---no lefs
than fix pieces were taken out by the probe on
the morning of Sept. 18, 1780,

> Nay, e'en in this unwelcome hour,
> When GOUT exerts its crippling pow'r,

He could not refift the itch for fcribbling.
" He *muft* have leave to fpeak that can't hold
" his tongue," fays the old proverb, " Though
" he does not know how to ftir his broth with-
" out fcalding his vinegar." Proud fpite and
burning envy, the perplexities of mind and
body, ftill kept poffeffion of his foul, and
yearn'd to try *one more fall* with the objects of
his hatred : and to this indifcretion was he pre-
cipitated by the fudden diffolution of Parliament; an epoch which furnifhed him with a
fpecious opportunity of difcharging that venom,
ex parte, which raged in him like the calen-
ture.

> " Where fhall the felf-tormented victim find
> " An antidote, to heal the poifon'd mind ?"

With the moft intemperate zeal, and with the
moft bare-faced apoftafy, did he imprecate an
oppofition to the very men, and meafures he
had

had, but a few years fince, efpoufed with a warmth bordering on madnefs! Hand-bills were dif- tributed *by his direction* in different parts of Nor- folk, ftrongly recommending the' fon of him who he had *grofly abufed* in 1768, to reprefent the county inftead of Mr. C-ke, whofe father and family he had *fupported* on three fimilar occa- fions : and this, not from any change of political fentiment *in them*, but from a vicious, malignant caprice *in him*—almoft inexplicable.

> " Much may it humble human nature's pride,
> " To mark how meanly HORACE chang'd his fide."

WITHOUT an ordinary portion of philofophic urbanity, nor actuated by the common-place maxims of religion and morality, our fcribbling- finner wantonly dared to trample on thofe leading points, friendfhip, honor, honefty ! and treat them as

> " Frolics, for men of fpirit only fit,
> " Where rapes are jefts, and murder is fheer wit."

WITH the moft fovereign contempt for every contingent that might militate to his advantage, and habituated to a lethargic foporific opiate, which had reduced the finer feelings of man to a vapid ftate, he gave a loofe to thofe latent fparks of poetic furor which difeafe, poverty, and contempt had, for a time, obfcured.

Not

Not the deep groans, the racking pains, `
- That round the couch of *ſickneſs* wait;
Not the ſharp ſting of cold *negleɕ*,
    The bitter taunt of peerleſs *hate*;
Not pining *ſorrow*'s weighty ſtroke,
Or *poverty*'s afflicting yoke :—

Not all theſe ills *united*, could 'move his cho-
ler! nor ſtay the viperous rancor of his pen!
Not all the twinges of the heart, nor aches of
the head, could wean him from the proſtitution of
thoſe intellectual abilities he ſo eminently poſſeſſed.
Whimſicallity and egotiſm are weak ſupporters
of an indifferent cauſe, yet DICK MERRY-FEL-
LOW ſaw not the fallacy of either, till it was too
late. The idea of mortifying Mr. C-ke, and Sir
H—d H—d, at this criſis, was to augur a re-
newal of life; but our hero, in this, as in
moſt things, *reckoned without his hoſt*; for
thoſe two gentlemen were re-choſen in a manner very honorable to themſelves, and their
conſtituents,

To effect his favourite purpoſe, DICK wrote
the following fragment of a poem, which,
amongſt ſome illiberal, and ſome incomprehen-
ſible ſallies of licentious wit, contains many juſt
remarks on the monopoly of the game.

A

A FRAGMENT of a POEM:

(Never before in print)

Addreſſed to the FREEHOLDERS OF NORFOLK, previous to the County Election;

On the MONOPOLY of the GAME:

By a FREEHOLDER.

*Non hic centauros, non gorgona, harpijſque
Juvenies, hominem pagina noſtra ſapit.*

MART.

Nor quail, nor partridge, is the Game I mind,
I ſhoot at MAN, and level at MANKIND.

- - - - - - - - - - - - -
- - - - - - - - - - - - -
- - - - - - - - - - - - -
- - - - - - - - - - - - -

How boaſts *Prince Pinery* the game he breeds !
That game, alas ! his ruin'd tenant feeds :
Let the poor man but whiſper, *he's undone*,
The keeper's ſent to take away his gun ;
Should hares and pheaſants ſpare the corn he grows,
He muſt not ſhoot, not even ſhoot—at crows.
The madman's hounds next take their ſummer-beat,
And hunt in *Auguſt* through the ſtanding wheat.
And O ! ye gods! ſhall this *baſhaw* be ſent
A ſenator to *Britain's* parliament,
There to preſerve our liberties and laws,—
A peerleſs guardian in his country's cauſe ?

But

But now, freeholders ! let your ftrength appear,
The year of liberty's—* the prefent year ;
Your turnips now are fafe, your corn may grow,
And hares and pheafants die in ev'ry row.
Let free-born principles direct your voice,
The man of fteady virtue be your choice :
Whofe public acts for fev'n years paft have fhewn—
He loves *your* welfare—as he loves his *own :*
Who courts your favor for no private end,
Whofe faith unfhaken, ne'er *forfook his friend*:
Like A—TL—y, has a mind of noble caft,
The fame good man in all his moment's paft :
Whofe heart is honeft, lads ! and in whofe eyes
Fair fame is more than all the game that flies :
Who, like a father, by his tenant ftands,
And fees a gun with patience in his hands.

- - - - - - - - - - - - - -
- - - - - - - - - - - - -

Let French invafions never fright your ear,
'Tis our *domeftic* tyrants we muft fear.
And fhall we fend them to the Commons' door
And arm them with frefh pow'r to hurt us more?
No, contrymen, be firm ! this year agree,
And fhew you have the courage—TO BE FREE:
Shew you difpife their low *feptennial* arts,—
Falfe promifes, falfe oaths, and falfe hearts :
Shew that you know them well ; and tho' before
You have been dup'd, you will be dup'd no more :
Be honeft to yourfelves ! fear no man's frown !
And as you fet them up, fo pull them down.

---

* The French fay, Englifhmen are *free* only fix weeks in
feven years; that is, during the time of a *general election.*

O

- - - - - - - - - - - - - - - •
- - - - - - - - - - - - - - -

Ne'er give a vote to *Growl's* tyrannic heir
Who makes you pay *five pounds* * to kill a hare :
Whose heart's fupremeft joy is to diftrefs,
See! harpy *Shylock* hov'ring o'er the PRESS : †
The printer's *devil* all his arts affail,
Then call him *poacher*, and he's fent to jail.
* But hark! what fhouts of joy ! the poll is o'er :
* And O ! Sir Growl's a fenator no more :
* Honor in THURLOW is the people's care,
* And fee ! a man of merit fills the chair.

---

* He made the landlord of an inn at *M· ncb-ft-r* (where he
is equally as refpedted as in *Norfolk)* pay 5l. for a hare that a
qualified gentleman gave him to drefs for a public company,
of which he was one : the gentleman ordered the landlord to
charge the hare in the dinner-bill 5l. which difcovered the
affair, on which *young Sir Growl* returned the money, and
abruptly left the room—in great confufion.

† Alludes to the attempt made at *Norwich*, two years ago,
to STOP THE LIBERTY OF THE PRESS, by *profeffed patriots.*

**** The four lines with afterifms were to be omitted, if
Sir H—— H—— came in for Norwich, and Mr. T—— loft
his election; and the following lines were to be added, after
—*his gown.* See next page, line 2.

But now triumphant fmiles on all he meets,
And mobs tumultuous—*drag him through the ftreets.*
Happy the man—O ! how completely bleft,
Whom all fupport, and yet whom all deteft !
When VIRTUE is no more the people's care,
WINDHAM muft fail, and THURLOW lofe the chair.

Grim

Grim look'd Sir *Growl*, as when afham'd to own
His brethren of the hall he caft his gown.

- - - - - - - - - - - - - - -
- - - - - - - - - - - - - - -

Once more to K-mb-rley recal your eyes,
And genuine worth in W-DEH--SE learn to prize :
Firft, at his country's call, to take the field,
The fpear to brandifh, or the fword to wield :
For him referve the honors of the ftate,
Honors, due only to the brave and great !

- - - - - - - - - - - - - - -
- - - - - - - - - - - - - - -

To D-rby fend the *Prince of Pines* away,
His father's friends to ruin or betray :
The wife indeed, are cautious to offend,
No foe fo deadly as an injur'd friend !
Deep in the coal-pits plunge the *Tufcan* down
To bring up colliers and parade the town;
To D-rby fend him back, where all agree
No coals nor colliers are fo black as he.
Proud, but yet mean, affecting L--c-ft-r's ftate,
Of foul too little, ever to be great !
Whom nor good faith nor gratitude could bind,
A hollow heart ! and a deceitful mind !
A difpofition grov'ling, bafe, and low,
While Arrogance fits louring on his brow !
His dogs are from his table fed,—the *poor* *
Are driv'n like flaves from his luxurious door :

---

* In the time of Lady L——r, the poor at H-lkh-m always
attended at the *Hall*, the morning after every *public day*, but
they have been forbid for two or three years paft, and the
remnants of prodigality have been given—to the hounds.

To

To focial joys by nature ne'er defign'd,
He only wants the pow'r to crufh mankind.—
WORTH MAKES, THE MAN ! on that we fix our eyes,
And fools we laugh at firft, and then defpife:
For know! in folly's wide eccentric round,
Meanefs and pride are oft together found.
Groaning for bricks, the hot-houfe walls, and inn
Stupendous ! force ev'n travellers to grin.—
- - - - - - - - - - - - - - - -
- - - - - - - - - - - - - - -

True greatnefs fprings from high defert alone,
Where virtue fails, 'tis loft upon a throne:
Of anceftors a long illuftrious race,
Where virtue fails, but adds to our difgrace:
The gilded palace, noife and nonfenfe rules,
And H—lkh-m Houfe becomes the neft of fools.
- - - - - - - - - - - - - - -
- - - - - - - - - - - - - -

See ! where he comes !—the precious *babe of grace !*
Bleft with a happy vacancy of face !
His fimp'ring tenants gather round and ftare,
His mouth fo open, and fo prim his air !
His mouth is open, but he is fo fhy
He never fpeaks—you know the reafon why—
No fenfe of honor nobly fpurs him on,
His hounds and horfes' his delight alone:
Feeling fo little for the worft difgrace,
He'd rather lofe his *feat*—than lofe a *chace:*
To fhew the *ruling paffion* of his foul,
His hounds and huntfmen muft attend the *poll:*
Th' election loft he cares not, fo the pack
Can find him out a fox in coming back:

Freeholders

. Freeholders, then, in time obſerve your cue !
And make as light of him as he of you.

- - - - - - - - - - - - - - ā
- - - - - - - - - - - - - - -

Worth, like Sir JOHN's*, ſhall merit your applauſe,
And W-NDH-M's eloquence protect our laws :
To men like theſe, ye ſons of NOLFOLK, look !
And laugh at all ſuch *Patriots* as C—.

SEPTEMBER 9, 1780.

THE election at Norwich for two citizens,
came on on Monday, September 11, when, after
a ſpirited exertion of the independent freemen,
to counteract the nefarious machinations of a few
leading men, the number of votes polled were
as follows :

Sir Harbord Harbord, Bart. of Gunſton   -   1382
Edward Bacon, Eſq. of Earlham,   -   1199
John Thurlow, Eſq. Alderman,   -   -   1103
William Windham, Eſq. of Felbrigg,   -   1069

IT is not to our purpoſe to enter into the merits
of this conteſt; we ſhall, therefore, only add, that
a more glorious ſtruggle to emancipate a large
and reſpectable body of citizens from the prevailing violation of their unalienable rights and
privileges, is not upon record !

_____

* Sir J-hn W-deh--fe of K-mb--ley.

O 3   THE

THE election of two knights of the shire to reprefent the county of Norfolk in parliament, came on at the Caftle of Norwich, on Wednefday, Sept. 20, when Sir Edward Aftley, Bart. of Melton-Conftable, and Thomas William Coke, Efq. of Holkham, were attended to the huftings by about two thoufand freeholders, and there chofen without oppofition!—to the great difappointment and mortification of our hero, who was all this time brooding over the influence his feeble efforts might have in the choice of members.

From the Cambridge Chronicle of Saturday, Nov. 25, 1780.

E P I G R A M.

Occafioned by the late Hue-and-Cry! after a Norfolk member at Weftminfter.

WHEN *C-rnw-ll* from Sir *Fl-tch-r* took the chair,
     Where were your m-mb-rs, *Norfolk*, tell us where?
Sir EDW-RD, truth it is, was in his place;
But where's your other m-mb-r?—At a *Race.*
The race for SPEAKERS?—No!—on *Swaffham* ground,
Running a match, was t'other m-mb-r found.
If fuch the object of the public voice,
Say, was not Norfolk *jockey'd* in her choice?
Or, when elections once more ftir the land,
Does C— for *Norfolk* or *Newmarket* ftand?

From

From the Morning Herald of Monday, November 20,
1780.

SIGHS *of the* SILVER DISHES *in a* CHEST *at a Banker's*
Shop in Norwich.

E P I G R A M.

"WE who fed princely L-c-ST-R and his bride;
" Now feed, alas ! the change, a Quaker's pride.
" New-fashion'd by a FOP, then pawn'd, or fold :
" Is the *new* fashion, better than the old ?"

From the Morning Herald of November 23, 1780.

CRUMBS *of* COMFORT *for the* SILVER DISHES
in a Chest at a Banker's shop in NORWICH.

In nova fert animus mutatas dicere formas
Corpora.——   OVID.

MOV'D by your fighs, dear DISHES ! let me bring
Peace to your minds upon my halcyon wing :
My name is HOPE—already fcenes arife
Fair for your fame before my wand'ring eyes.—
What were you at the princely L—c—ft—r's feaft ?
Mere minifters of luxury at beft—
Difgraceful ftate for your intrinfic worth !
Now fober Juftice brings your merit forth ;
And in juft recompence has giv'n you pow'r
To feed upon HIS heir, WHO fed on you before.
It is not pride—I fpeak this to your fhame—
But modeft five-per-cent's the QUAKER's aim.
To fhield your crefts and fhining fides from blows
And Ifralitifh fweats the law allows

.   O 4   This

'This juſt reward; and, ſure I am, my *friend* *
Will for the law effect its nobleſt end:
But if hard-hearted C-KE † full many a year
Perſiſts in thinking you beneath his care;
The faithful ‡ Naſmith ſhall at laſt convey
Your forms, uninjur'd, through a length of way,
To happier Southern climes, whoſe genial flames
Shall make you perfect on the banks of Thames.
Stamp'd with the image, by a ſkilful hand,
Of the lov'd, pitied, ruler of the land;
All! all! ſhall then confeſs your uſe and pow'r;
The wiſe ſhall court you, and the fool adore.
But in your various viſits thro' the town—
Fail not—'tis on the peril of my frown—
To call at fam'd Craig's-court—now mind my word—
'Tis on your left hand up, at door the third—
There ſhall you find the tuner of the lay;
O! crown him with a better crown than bay!
So ſhall the headlong multitude for you
Join the calm plaudits of the virtuous few;
And, ſpite of epigrams, or ſung, or told,
" NEW FASHIONS ſhall be better than the OLD."

---

* The Banker at Norwich.
† Suppoſed to be meant by the fop.—See Epigram.
‡ A good old true-blue Whig carrier.

From

[201]

From the Morning Herald of Saturday, November 25, 1780.

L I N E S,
Written on a Window, near a Banker's Shop in
NORWICH.

O! May the *orange-colour'd* fool I hate,
Affect to live in grandeur and in ftate,
While banker's clerks beftride his mortgag'd plate
Lumb'ring the fhop, imprifon'd in a cheft,
To all who enter,—a true *ftanding* jeft.

From the Cambridge Chronicle of Saturday, December
23, 1780.

E P I G R A M,

On a Norwich Alderman's exciting the mob pro-
fanely out of Scripture, " to fetch their King*
back," at the late election.

TEXT-Murd'ring *Crocus*, circl'd in a ring,
Bawls out, " Go, Norwich men ! bring back your
King."
" 'Tis what we wifh," replies an honeft JAC,
" We wifh to bring *our little Ch-rley back*."

---

* Sir H-rb-rd, who had *abdicated* and was gone.

The

The COURSE: A Song.

Addreſſed to the GENTLEMEN of the
NORFOLK COURSING MEETING.

NO more let wine, no more let hounds,
    Engage the tuneful Nine:
I chuſe a theme beyond them all;
    The Courſe, the Courſe be mine.
        Then a courſing we will go,
        Then a courſing we will go, will go,
        And a courſing we will go.

The well-breath'd greyhound o'er the plain,
    Had long ago been ſung;
But dreading the exalted theme,
    Each poet held his tongue.
        Then a courſing, &c.

The hunter who purſues his game,
    From earlieſt dawn till noon,
Laughs at the courſer's rapid joy,
    Becauſe 'tis o'er too ſoon.
        Then a courſing, &c.

But is there not, my friends, a bliſs
    Extatic as the Courſe,
Of which no one has ſaid, as yet,
    For ſhortneſs 'tis the worſe.
        Then a courſing, &c.

Let

Let thofe who think the Courfe is dull,
  Attend at beauty's fhrine,
Where TOWNSHEND, PEYTON, grace the plain,
  And make the fport divine.
      Then a courfing, &c.

Whether on *Weeting's* well-kept field,
  Or HAMOND's wide domain;
Or at the ftouter hares on *Smee*,
  Witch, Quince, and Laura ftrain.
      Then a courfing, &c.

Or upon *Stonehinge's* bounding turf,
  Which e'en with *Norfolk* vies;
Or over ASTLEY's well-ftock'd heaths,
  The Wiltfhire greyhound flies.
      Then a courfing, &c.

How much mifnam'd the Courfe by thofe
  Who beat each hedge with care;
And pleas'd, if in the live-long day,
  They kill one haplefs hare.
      Then a courfing, &c.

No, let me fee the well-train'd dogs,
  In VALE's unerring hand,
Loos'd at an inftant from the flips,
  And fkimming o'er the land.
      Then a courfing, &c.

With ORFORD of the gallant train,
  Defervedly the pride,
His friends around him gladly throng,
  By worth, by fport, allied.
      Then a courfing, &c.

Thus

Thus meet my friends, and twice each year
Renew the charming fport;
And whilft we've health and ftrength, my lads!
Let's pufh about the port. .

    Then a drinking, &c.

Then fill each glafs, a bumper fill;
No day-light be there found :
Drink, drink the Courfe; halloo! my boys!
And let the toaft go round.

    Then a courfing, &c.

ADVERTISEMENT,

From the Cambridge Chronicle, Jan. 13, 1781.

In the month of February, 1781, will be publifhed,

The Difappointed WIFE *of* NORFOLK :
Or, the Drunken Phyfician ordering a feparate Bed.

O H ! that I had but remain'd a widow !
 All is not gold that glitters!
It is a fad thing to have a nominal hufband !

From the Cambridge Chronicle, January 20, 1781.

EPIGRAM,

On letters to the printer being charged, in Croufe's Norfolk Chronicle, as advertifements, by the Stamp-Office
at Norwich.

S WORN foe to the prefs, like moft of his betters,
 Old *Shylock* now *fqueezes* a duty on letters?

          " Of

" Of what ufe are *letters*, exclaims the old *Jew*,
" Unlefs C—ke and H—rb—d their alphabet knew ?
" But if *Croufe* prints *new* letters, I'll forfeit my head,
" For I'll mark them with EADEM SEMPER* in *red !*"

E P I G R A M,

On hearing of a late intended *duel in Hyde-Park.*

THE TALL MAN of London, of prowefs fo ftout,
Lo ! fends to a *Juftice of Peace*—when called out:
" And 'twas right," cries Sir *Growl*, " what can a man do ?
" I *once* was *called out*, and I fent unto *two*."

E P I T A P H on a C A T,

That always begged when he faw any body eat.

DICK, when *alive*, gave joy to me,
And comfort to the poor now *dead* ;
Since nothing fatter was than he,
And yet he always—*begg'd his bread.*
Hunftanton Cliff. ORLANDO.

IN this rotundancy of poetic amufement did
our hero move ; giving, as he thought, a *coup
d'œil* by every line ; and although it cannot be
faid of him, as *Erafums* fpeaks of *Skelton* the
poet-lauret to Henry VIII. that he was " the
" light and honor of the Britifh learning,"
Britannicarum literarum lumem et decus, yet he was

---

* Motto on the ftamp.

by

by no means an inelegant writer. He was not
the *ftricken deer* who fheds his tears in folitude
and filence, nor the *phænix* of the feâ of Zeno ;
his rhymes were rattles for children of a larger
growth ; and the difcovery of the longitude, or
the philofopher's ftone, nay, what is more proble-
matical than either, the liquidation of the national debt, would have been an eafier tafk to
him, than a prohibition of this *play thing.*

Irony is undoubtedly the keeneft weapon of
fatire, but laughter is bought too dear, if it be
at the expence of decency ; and " want of de-
" cency, is want of fenfe." Like the monfter
furious with a hundred heads,—*Bellua Centiceps,*
of Horace, he grinned forth perfonal invective with the moft provoking vivacity and affec-
tation of pleafantry. Pertinacious, vehement, invidious, impetuous, and fomewhat ambidextrous,
with penetration and ftrong natural abilities, we
can give thofe perfons, incurring his diflike,
credit, who exclaim with *Horace,*

Vefanum tetigiffe timent fugiuntque poetam.

Fly ! neighbours, fly ! he raves ; his verfes fhow it;
Fly ! or you're caught, you're bit—by a mad poet.

As Dr. *Fuller* fays, " if he was *ingenious* he was
not *ingenuous*; to every pound of wit he had hardly
a drachm of good nature :" yet he had learning
                                        fufficient

fufficient to tell a *Lexicon* from a *Latin Bible* : and,
though we cannot rank him with *Ariſtippus*
amongſt courtiers and philoſophers, whoſe character is ſo finely and ſo juſtly drawn in one beautiful line by HORACE,

> *Omnis Ariſtippum decuit color, et ſtatus, et res.*

He had duplicity enough to ſuit himſelf to the
tempers and capacities of thoſe *few* who continued to liſten to *his tale of woe* ; but, *audi al-
teram partem*, one ſtory is good till another be
told. When Philip of Macedon ſat in judgment, he uſed to ſtop one ear, which, he ſaid,
he reſerved for the defendant. This is an excellent rule, with reſpect to the different parties
in all ſubjects of controverſy and litigation. By
ſuppreſſing ſome circumſtances, and artfully
varniſhing others, falſehood may be made to bear
the ſemblance of truth.

> —— *Hic niger eſt : hunc tu, Romane, caveto.*
>
> HOR.

This man's a knave ; therefore beware of him.

> CREECH.

THE truth is, our hero either wanted ſaga-
city to diſcover the ſtrength of the power he
provoked, or he had not virtue enough to decline a conteſt : maintaining, that a blot at back-
gammon

[208]

gammon, is no blot—till hit. With Voltaire's
Candide, " All is for the beſt ;" and, with
our favorite Engliſh bard, " What ever is, is
right."

---

*From the Norfolk Chronicle of Saturday, January 27,
1781.*

To the Memory of Miſs TRYON.

SMOOTH run the verſe that decks *Maria's* bier,
True as her worth, and as my grief ſincere.
Faſt flow the tears which fill *Maria's* grave ;
Where friendſhip weeps, ſure haplefs love will rave !
For Oh ! how oft' to rapture did ſhe move
The ear of friendſhip and the eye of love!
How oft her wit, with winning ſmiles diſplay'd,
Secur'd the conqueſt that her charms had made !
Cold are thoſe limbs !—loſt is that power to pleaſe
With faultlefs form and unaffected eaſe !
Vain youth ! 'tis yours, to kindle with your breath
The lamp of Hymen, or the torch of death.
Yet ſtill to ſoothe (if ought can ſoothe our woes)
At friendſhip's call the faithful canvafs* glows.
Mark well yon portrait !—let the pleaſing pain
Throb in each breaſt, and thrill thro' every vein.
Such *were* the features, that we all admir'd !
Such *was* the air, that nature's ſelf inſpir'd—
Here then her new exiſtence we will date,
For *here* ſhe lives beyond the power of fate.

---

* A portrait of Miſs TRYON.

THESE

THESE pathetic lines were wrote by Mr. MERRY-FELLOW to the memory of a young lady, who died whilſt on a viſit to Edmund Rolfe, Eſq. at Heacham, four miles from *M—t-A—a.* Youth and beauty had a charm to move the *tender* feeling, which even the honors of grey hairs and age could not reſiſt.

" Yet, what we can't deſcribe, we may adore ;
" The gods allow us this,—and aſk no more."

————————

To the PRINTER *of the* NORFOLK CHRONICLE.

SIR,

THE illiberal and unjuſt ſtrictures on the much-admired rural poem of SEPTEMBER, that were exhibited in the *Critical Review* of laſt month, are a freſh conviction how little the public can depend upon the character given of any performance by the writers of that miſerable compilation : indeed, for the moſt part, judicious readers are inclined to purchaſe a new work more readily if they ſee it condemned in the *Review*, as moſt probably the performance is not without a great deal of merit ; their cenſures are frequently found malicious and falſe, and to a degree ridiculous : ſo ridiculous indeed, that many people are of opinion, that they ſeldom read beyond the *title-page* of the work they criticiſe : where they *do* read farther, they appear illiterate beyond meaſure, and of courſe are ſure to miſrepreſent the author whom they do not underſtand.

P   But

But a more glaring mifreprefentation of any performance was never feen than what they have given of the
poem in queftion, where as much true humor and wit,
and juft fatire upon the inordinate paffion for the *monopoly
of game,* fo prevalent amongft our *country'Squires,* has been
difplayed, as this age has produced; wrote with great
eafe, and in defiance of all *reviewers,* in the true " fpirit
of poetry." But to their remarks :

" The frefh-fhorn fields, and *covies* proud of wing :
" The pointers leaping at their mafter's fide.
" And *full-blown* fportfmen in their autumn pride."

" The defcription of thofe *full-blown* fportfmen with their
many diverting pranks forms the *whole bufinefs* of this important work." The main objeft of the poem is to ridicule an exceffive paffion for game; to indulge which,
many gentlemen of very amiable qualities in other refpeéts
fully a reputation that would acquire them the love of
mankind, and who, though the greateft poachers themfelves, become tyrants to all the neighbourhood about
them ; the poet endeavours to laugh them out of it : he
holds up a *glafs,* but the misfortune is, that if *twenty*
look in it at once, a man fees every body's face *but his
own.*

" *Covies* proud of wing."

Notwithftanding the farcaftical italics of the *reviewers,*
is a proper and very poetical expreffion :

Infolitos docuere Nifus.   HOR.

" *Comus,* dear droll ! hold both thy fides and fee
" Decripit threefcore *turnip'd* to the knee."

Turnip'd

Turnip'd to the knee, is very defcriptive in this paffage : it is not only intelligible to the *meaneft capacity*, though the reviewers fay, " it is far beyond our comprehenfion," but the painting is ftrong; the whole paffage indeed is beautiful, and a juft ridicule upon *old fportfmen*, who pur- fue the diverfions of the field beyond their years and ftrength.

If in *feven* hundred lines, not *two or three* hundred, as mentioned by the reviewers, (an inftance of their great accuracy and attention to the work before them) they could only *pick* out *two* expreffions to find fault with, it is fubmitted to all impartial judges, who know how ready they are to find fault, whether it is not a fair prefump- tion, that the poem in queftion has no fmall degree of merit.

I am yours, &c.

Dec. 30, 1780.   C A N D O R.

P. S. In the very next page to their remaks on *Sep- tember*, the reviewers quote the following line from *Horace*,

    " *Difficile eft proprie communia dicere.*"——

They render *communia*, old, " *hackneyed*" fubjects, whereas the poet meant directly the contrary : fubjects that had never been handled before, that lay as it were *in common* for any man to take up! that had never been touched upon :

Avia pieridum peragro loca, NULLIUS ANTE
TRITA PEDE.————   LUCR.

P 2   This

This was evidently the meaning of *Horace* In the word *communia*: such subjects as Gay's *Trivia*, Pope's *Rape of the Lock*, Congreve's *Ben the Sailor*, &c. The whole passage shews it plainly : *Horace* says, in his instructions to *Dramatic* poets, and it is to the drama this quotation from the poet is applied (the farce of " The humors of an Election.")

> Si quid *inexpertum* scenæ committis, et audes
> Personam formare *novam*, servetur ad imum
> Qualis ab incæpto procefferit et sibi conftat;
> " Difficile.eft proprie *communia* dicere," tu que
> Rectius Iliacum carmen deducis in actus
> Quam si proferres *ignota indictaque primus:*

Can any thing be more plain than the meaning of *Horace?* but you, reviewers, render *communia*, " hackneyed" subjects :

> *En! Quales sitis* JUDICES!   PHOEDRUS.

It is pleasant sometimes, to read the diversity of opinions of the temporary critics. The Monthly Review speaks very handsomely of the poem of *September*; the *Critical* Reviewers declare, there is not one good line in the whole poem !

The above *critique on the critics* is a *friendly* and able defence of a poem, written by the Revd. J-rm-n Pr-tt of W-tlingt-n in Norfolk, who has honeftly, very properly, and with forcible arguments, exposed the absurdity and folly of pursuing the feathered *game* with that tenacious, inflexible, sanguinary difpofition, so prevalent among

among the lords of manors—of all ranks and
ages ! complexions and fizes !

" Without a mind a MAN is but an ape,
" A mere brute body—in a human fhape."

THE tenuity of this puerile and trivial paffion
for *cruelty** is ranked, among the votaries of TASTE,
as the compendium or *fummum bonum* of human
perfection. The vague and indeterminate gufto
among jockeys and hunters of the higher clafs
hath found its way into *St. Stephen's Chapel,* where
you'll find the *ins* and the *outs*—in the drefs and
toils of *Newmarket.*

" Go on, brave youths ! till in fome future age
" *Whips* fhall become the fenatorial badge;
" 'Til ENGLAND fee her *jockey* fenators
" Meet all at Weftminfter—in boots and fpurs ;
" See the whole houfe, with mutual frenzy mad,
" Her patriots all—in *leathern* breeches clad ;
" Of *bets*—not taxes, learnedly debate,
" And guide with equal reins—a *fteed* and ftate."

WARTON.

To the *extreme* relifh for the field and turf
may be added, the mental quixotifm of the cabinet *connoiffeurs* among pictures, books, prints,
coins, relics, ftatues, terraffes, ha-ha's, and a

---

* HOGARTH's Stages. Horfe-racing, cock-fighting, bull-
baiting, fox-hunting, courfing, fhooting, hawking, fifhing,
driving, boxing, dueling, &c.

P 3   thoufand

thoufand whimfical *et cetera's* which come under
the denomination of *Tafte.*

    " Bleft age ! when all men may procure
    " The title of a *Connoiſſour.*
    " When noble and ignoble herd
    " Are govern'd by a fingle word ;
    " Though, like the royal *German* dames,
    " It bears an hundred Chriftian names ;
    " As Genius, Fancy, Judgment, *Goût,*
    " Whim, Caprice, *Je-ne-ſcai-quoi, Virtù :*
    " Which appellations all defcribe
    " TASTE, and the modern *tafteful* tribe.

                         Mr. TOWN.

From the Morning Herald of Friday, March 9, 1781.

E P I G R A M,

On the *Scotch Rebels* flying from the late Duke of
CUMBERLAND, into Derbyfhire, in 1745.

Written by an Officer.

COPE, when the rebel troops were near at hand,
   Took to the *ſea* to fight 'em on the *land :*
WADE, better thought he could not be too near,
And fo kept clofe *behind* the *Chevalier.*
But the brave *Duke,* with many a gallant boy,
That fear'd not fire nor fword at *Fontenoy,*
Struck terror to the youth in one fhort week,
And drove him—to the *Devil's-Arſe-a-Peak!*

                             THE

THE following *epilogue* and *song*, were written by DICK, MERRY-FELLOW, under the moſt excruciating pangs of the gout. His mind poſſeſſed a vigor and brilliancy of conceit, which neither difeafe, chagrine, embarraſſment, reflection, nor the *maigre* ſupport of panado, could damp. Pride is an ingredient in the compoſition of ſome men, which will buoy them up in a ſea of trouble. The *frog-glutton* of the land of croakers, and the *two-legg'd conſumer of oats* of the land of cakes, are, in the words of JUVENAL,

———— ———*Vivimus ambitioſâ*
Paupertate.————

EVERY ſtate of life, from the loweſt peaſant to the higheſt ſovereign, has its ſorrows and diſappointments, and the moſt rigid virtue is not infallible. Vice is a gradual and eaſy deſcent; and it requires more ſublimity of thought than comes to the ſhare of many, to recover the ineſtimable bleſſing of happineſs and peace, by contrition and imploring mercy,

Hos diri conſcia faƐli
Mens habet attonitos et ſurdo verbere cædit
Occultum quatiente animo tortore flagellum.

JUV. Sat. 13.

Not ſharp revenge, nor hell itſelf can find,
A fiercer torment than a guilty mind;

P 4   Which

Which day and night doth dreadfully accufe,—
Condemns the wretch, and ftill the charge renews.

CREECH's Juvenal, Sat. 13.

———— ———— a time
Will come, (enquire not how) this is enough;
'Tis plain : a time there will be after death,
When God, as fit, the juft from the unjuft,
The guiltlefs from the guilty will feleƈt,
And give to ev'ry man his due reward.

Dr. GREY's tranflation.

WE do not mean to apply thefe fententious gleanings to our hero *alone:*—Let he whom the cap fits, wear it; for, with the poet, DICK ufed to. fay,

Let the gall'd jade go winch,
My withers are unwrung :————

An OCCASIONAL EPILOGUE,

To the Tragedy of CYMBELINE, *performed by Gentle-men, at the Theatre at* LYNN-REGIS *in Norfolk, on Eafter-Monday, April 16, 1781 ; for the benefit of the company of Comedians.*

Spoken by Mrs. KING, *in the Charaĉter of* IMOGEN.

SO ! gentlemen *again* * upon the ftage !
O ! when will ceafe this rank THEATRIC rage?
See ! foldiers† ! fportfmen ! all the humor fuits,
And tragic *bufkins* triumph over *boots !*
O ! where is now that *fury* for the chace,
That erft inflam'd old NIMROD's iron race?
Turn'd *players* all, however ftrange the faĉt !
But yet we never fee their *ladies* aĉt :
And fome, perhaps, it might not greatly vex,
Like *Imogen,* for *once* to change their fex :
To wear th' apparel, tho' but for an *hour,*
That conftitutes o'er man fuch *magic* pow'r ;
If *once put on,* it fometimes lafts *for life,*
And the *fierce hufband* grows a *pliant wife !*
Dear *ladies,* try the drefs, and never fear it,
For fome are thought, and fome are *known* to wear it ‡
Come, one and all, and at the *Green-room* meet—
You know our play-houfe ftands in *Chequer-ftreet* ‡.

---

* Alludes to the Comedy of the " Clandeftine Marriage." performed by *Gentlemen* at the Lynn theatre, on Monday, March 22, 1779, and another play in 1780.

† Officers of the Eaft Effex militia, and gentlemen whó played the principle parts.

‡ Long diftinguifhed in Lynn, as the quarter of the *Grays.*

Why,

Why, what a mad vain-glorious *mate* had I,
My faith acrofs the CONTINENT to try !
Send an *Italian* too ! to find me out ?
—Choice lovers came from *Italy* no doubt !
The *gentle* youth did not *difturb* my reft,
Content to *view*—the *mole upon my breaft:*
O ! had a *turban'd* TURK come in his ftead,
Who cou'd have anfwer'd for a *virgin's* bed ?

Then I muft take a trip, poor fool, to WALES:
—I've heard a *trip to* SCOTLAND feldom fails.
But who would change *cork*-hoops and petticoats,
To ramble 'mongft caves, and rocks, and goats?
Or *mountaineers*, to beauty BOTH fo blind ?
The *brutes* could not diftinguifh *woman-kind.*
Had I from *Milford* crofs'd the *Irifh* main,
Hat, coat, and fword, had been put on in vain :
To thofe bright fons of *gallantry* and arms,
No drefs had *long* conceal'd—a WOMAN's charms !

Our play to-night corrects th' *hiftoric* page,
That gives up *Albion's* cliffs to Roman rage :
Our fea-girt ISLE difdains a foreign foe,
This *Romans* knew, and *French* and *Spaniards* know.
GEORGE, like another *Cymbeline*, commands,
And heads as warlike and victorious bands :
Alike prepar'd to humble, or chaftife,
France in arms, or treacherous *allies:*
Whilft vengeance on their pow'rs *combin'd* is hurl'd,
His thunders fhake th' affrighted *weftern* world.
No diftant fubject *unredrefs'd* complains,
While RODNEY conquers, and while BRUNSWIC reigns.

The

The STRONG BEER of *Old England:* or, The JOLLY TARS of LYNN.

A New Occasional Ballad.

Sung upon the Theatre at Lynn-Regis in Nor-folk, by Mr. HERBERT, in the Character of *Congreve's* BEN THE SAILOR, April 16, 1781.

To the Tune of, "O! the ROAST BEEF of Old England," &c.

COME, *mefs-mates*, be jolly, and drive away care,
A fig for the DON, and a fig for MYNHEER!
Come, take off a Can of Old Englifh STRONG BEER.
O! the ftrong Beer of Old England,
And O! the Old Englifh ftrong beer.

True friendfhip and honefty pleafure imparts,
No COURTIERS are here with their fycophant arts,
To *fmile* on the man whom they *hate* in their hearts.
O! the ftrong beer, &c.

No PARLIAMENT-MAN, who with cant and grimace,
Will give you ftrong beer—till he gets into *place,*
And then, like a churl, *throws his door* in your face.
O! the ftrong beer, &c.

Brave DRAKE, round the world, what enabled to fteer,
And make *Spain, France,* and *Portugal* tremble with fear?
—Why, he din'd off ROAST BEEF, and drank nothing but BEER.
O! the roaft beef, &c.

In

In London, *French* cooks and *French* turtles abound,
But where is the PARLEZ-VOUS cook to be found,
Like the BRITON, who knocks a fat OX to the ground ?
          O! the roaſt beef, &c.

Your FOREIGN-BRED *Engliſhman* turns up his noſe
At a horn of OLD STINGO, too potent for *beaux,*
It may ſtrain his weak nerves, or may ſpot his lac'd cloaths.
          O! the ſtrong beer, &c.

Let the *French* on our coaſt preſume to appear,
Our MILITIA ſhall ſhew them the pow'r of beer,
Their *frogs* and *ſoup-maigre* will never do here.
          O! the ſtrong beer, &c.

Old VERNON we honor for giving us GROG,
To heave up our anchor, and heave out our log,
But what's to compare with a can of GOOD NOG?
          O! the ſtrong beer, &c.

Here's a health to brave RODNEY, and all his brave tars!
Who fight like old Britons in ſpite of old ſcars,
And make the *Van-Berkel's* to hang down their ears !
          O! the ſtrong beer, &c.

Let's never forget in his age and retreat,
THE MAN, who the *Monſieurs* ſo DRUBB'D and ſo beat,
Here's a health to Ld. HAWKE ! and ſucceſs to the FLEET!
          O! the ſtrong beer, &c.

Let Shuldham, Howe, Keppel, and Harland ſo brave,
Roſs, Campbell, and Barrington, ſtem the proud wave,
For theſe are the men that our country muſt SAVE.
          O! the ſtrong beer, &c.

STRONG

STRONG BEER made our fore-fathers hardy and bold,
STRONG BEER makes the fons like their fathers of old !
All *true Englifh hearts* love it better than GOLD.
                              O! the ftrong beer, &c.

See ! HENRY, young Prince, to all *feamen* fo dear,
What makes him fo ftout, fuch a ftranger to fear ?—
—His *tea-cup* he chang'd for a CUP OF STRONG BEER.
                              O ! the ftrong beer, &c.

May KING GEORGE live for ever, he can't live too long !
May his STEERSMAN know always the right from the
      wrong !
And may all LOYAL SUBJECTS drink nothing but STRONG !
                              O ! the ftrong beer, &c.

WE are now drawing to the moft awful period
of our heroe's exiftence. A few months of time
will emancipate him from a ftate of body and
mind,

      " Like fad Prometheus, thus to lie,
      " In endlefs pain, and never die.

YET, ever amidft the horrors of a couch, and
impending ruin! " When cares oppreffive rack
the troubled foul ;" he felt the fame itch for
fcribbling as if he had had a falvo in his pocket
for every evil ; and was momentoufly engaged
in a work, of which the following is his advertifement, taken from the *Cambridge Chronicle* of
Auguft 25, 1780.

                                                In

[222]

In the press, and speedily will be published, in 8vo.

THE NAVAL REGISTER; or, An Historical Account, from authentic records and papers, of the most remarkable sea-engagements, expeditions, attacks, and sieges, and a complete list of squadrons and commanders, from the year 1739 to the present year 1781. To be annually published on the 1st of May, during the continuance of the present hostilities, or war of reprisals. To which will be added an appendix, containing a list of the Admirals, Captains, Lieutenants, and ships in commission of the royal navy of England, arranged and formed upon an entire new plan: with a list of the royal navies of England, France, and Spain, during the wars of 1740 and 1756, and an accurate account of the number of line-of-battle ships of France and Spain, now in commission.

By R-CH-RD G-RD-N-R, Esq.

Captain of Marines on board his Majesty's ship the Rippon of 60 guns in the last war, and author of " The Account of an Expedition against Martinico, Guadelupe, and other the Caribbee Islands in the West-Indies in 1759," dedicated, by permission, to the Queen.

——— Versas ad Littora Puppes
Respiciunt, totumque allabi Classibus Æquor.——Virg.

—————————Imperi
Porrecta Majestas ab Ortu
Solis ad Hesperium Cubile
Custode Rerum Cæsare.———Hor.

Lynn, printed by W. Whittingham, and sold by J. Fielding, London.

PART

PART of the copy of this work was put into the hands of a printer at Lynn-Regis, who
had done some of it at press, when Mr. MERRY-
FELLOW died. By so premature an exit, the
public, we fear, will be deprived of the benefit
of his labors on a subject so very important
at this juncture, and the printer suffer a consider-
able loss.

A T this time, our hero had also a poem,
called *The* TRIPPING JURY; *a Norfolk Tale:*
inscribed to Sir H-rb-rd H-rb-rd, Bart. Member for
Norwich, which he published soon after, at one
shilling. The *advertisement to the reader* is a direct libel on T. W. C-ke, Esq. and the *dedication*
to Sir H. H. is a malicious attempt at irony :
alluding to the *manner* of his being re-chosen
member for Norwich, on the ever-memorable
11th of September, 1780. but falsly and ænig-
matically related.

TRIPPING

TRIPPING a-là-Mode:

An Assemblage of Hudibrasticks.

Ludere par Impar.—— HOR.

By DICK MERRY-FELLOW, Esq.

OF MOUNT-VESUVIUS.

LOCK'D up for hours forty-eight,
A *N-rf-lk* juryman of late,
Depriv'd of meat, and drink, and fire,
And almoſt ready to expire :
" A plague ! ſhall nine of us, cries he,
" Be ſtarv'd to death for two or three,
" Becauſe the *dumplins* won't agree ?
" Why, look'ye, honeſt neighbours, look !
" They're all as head-ſtrong as 'Squire C—
" As head-ſtrong did I ſay, nay more,
" I might have ſaid,—almoſt as *poor* ;
" And none to judge are at a loſs,
" How want of money makes us croſs :
" 'Twas that, I'll hold you any wager,
" That made C-KE quarrel with the *Major.*
" With open mouth, ſee ! how they ſtare
" And gape—like L-c-ſt-r's *gapping* hair ;
" By *Shylock* ſent to th' bank too late
" To take a peep at his own plate* :

---

* Alludes to a ſuperb ſervice of plate *ſent from home* in this time of war, and danger of *privateers*, to a banker's ſhop at Norwch,—*for ſecurity.*

" Who

" Who fooner, on the *N-rf-lk* coaft,
" Runs me his head againft a poft ?
" And what he gets into his brain
" The *Dev'l* can ne'er get out again :
" Like table hunting JACK of *Cl-y*,
" *Wriggling his head*, as who fhould cry,
" *There's none of you fo wife as I?*
" No, not amongft you all is one,
" Not ev'n Count L—, the hatter's fon ;
" Nor he, caft forth of the fame mother,
" That lout, his *Common*-ftealing brother.
" Nor *genius* of the law-run-mad,
" *Cream*-colour'd *Ciceronian* CH—D.
" Nor he, that nervous *G-nt-n* finner,
" Who on a *lev'ret* fed at dinner,
" But made the honeft *landlord* pay
" *Five pounds* before he went away :
" Five pounds ! for what ? O ! droll to name,—
" For killing hares—For killing game ?
" But had it been a precious pheafant,
" He found it was his *Worfhip's* prefent.
" A neighb'ring hofpitable *'Squire*,
" Who waxing hot, and full of ire ;
" Sir *Growl* turn'd pale, *runs to a friend*,
" (His *ufual way*, his *fcrapes to end* ;)
" Then left the company to dine,
" * Sneak'd down ftairs, and return'd the *fine :*
" The *'Squire*, who faw he would not fight †,
" Call'd after him," " Sir *Growl*, good night !"

---

* See journals of the gentleman's club at M-nch-ft-r.
† See Major G-rd-n-r's letter to Sir H-rb d H-rb-rd, Bart.
ditto to Th-m-s W-ll--m C-ke, Efq. 1778.

Q   " Good

" Good night, Sir *Growl!*—The waiters cry,
" And merry footmen ftanding by.
" But to return—for his difgreffion,
" You'll pardon me on my conceffion.
" Why, honeft neighbours, look-ye here !
" Would it not make a parfon fwear
" To fee thefe three C—KE-headed loobies,
" What, not a word, ye H-lkh-m boobies?
" —Sirs, if you mean to-night to fup,
" Come, for a *verdict* let's *trip up* * :
" This finifhes at once difputes,—
" The only way to deal with *brutes.*

Our tale, tho' ftrange, we muft proceed;
No fooner fpoke, than all agreed :
Up went the *fhilling*, difcord healing,
Down came the verdict from the *cieling :*
" Look, gentlemen, and fee it light,
" An even chance but what 'tis right ;
" So—now the fquabbling *plaintiff*'s undone,
" And my Lord *Judge* may *trip* for *London.*"

Who laughs at this our ftory, who ?
Laugh as you pleafe, but it is true †;
And was the fyftem underftood,
It might be for the nation's good :
What but the *fhilling*, where it falls,
Brings peace into *St. Stephen's* walls ?

---

* *Tofs up*, with a half-penny, fhilling, or any other coin,
and not to make a *falfe ftep*, as *tripping* is generally underftood.—*deprebendo.*
    † An actual fact, at an affize at Norwich.

If that a fhilling from the throne
Tofs'd up aloft fhould tumble down,
Say, *grumblers*, where's the man not willing
In times like thefe—to *turn a fhilling* ?
The YANKEES, tho' fo proud of late,
A fhilling turn'd, might turn their fate;
Nor would it their high fpirits damp
To turn it,—tho' it bore a *ftamp*.
Up with the *fhilling*, down goes pride,
Thro' realms extended far and wide;
For while the fhilling's in the air,
See! *Dutchmen, Frenchmen, Spaniards* ftare;
Eager to know the chance may hap,
Each holds and ftretches out his cap.

O! what a great expence of blood
Might *Britain* fave in many a wood;
On many a tent-environ'd plain,
Where thoufands in a day are flain:
If e'er the guns began to rattle,
CORNWALLIS *tripp'd up* for the battle.

What endlefs treaties, negociations,
Might well be fpar'd contending nations,
If that *hoftilities* might ceafe,
The POW'RS AT WAR—*tripp'd up* for PEACE.

When fleets combin'd of *France* and *Spain*,
Pop *out* and then pop *in* again;
What better fchemes could *Fleury* † hit on
Than let them both *trip up* for *Britain* ?

---

† Monfieur JOLI DE FLEURY, fucceffor to the great French
financier, Monfieur NECKAR.

Q 2   Or

Or force the Dutch on 'Statia's high-land,
To *trip* with R**odney** for the Island?

   Port-Praya's tar *, who cannot *write*,
Swears he'll make all his *Captains* fight;
For *Frenchmen* cares not he a button,—
So he can lay the blame on *S-tt-n.*
Ships without mafts, we all agree,
May eafily—be *tow'd* to fea ;
Was he not favage as a cannibal,
He might have *tripp'd up* for th' *Hannibal* ;
It fure had been a better thing,
And pleas'd the nation—and the K**ing**.

   But not too far abroad to roam,
Let's bring our fyftem nearer home ;
Would candidates have one objection
To *trip* for feats at an election ?
When there are hundreds, you and I know,
So glad to fave their ready *rhino* ?
Nay e'en Sir E**dward**'s † perpetuity
Might *trip* to fave a fmall gratuity,—
Since there is nought to *trip withal*
At G-nt-n—or at H-lkh-m Hall ?

   How near had F-x* and B-**rke** † of late
Tripp'd up our Minifters of State,

---

  * Commodore J-hnft-n : fee his letter in the London Gazette.
  † Sir Ed--rd A-tl-y, Bart. member for N-rf-lk, brought in
the bill to render " perpetual" the late Mr. Grenville's
election-bill.
   * Hon. Ch--les J-mes, F-x, reprefentative for Weftminfter.
  † Edm--d B-rke, Efq. member for Malton in Yorkfhire.

                                Tho'

Tho' had they all come tumbling down,
Such is " THE POWER of the CROWN,"
In fpite of D-NN-NG.*, fpite of B—RE, †
Or fchemes form'd only to mifcarry,
Twenty to one it would have been
If e'er a *Patriot* got in.

N-RTH ‡ in his life ne'er brighter fhone
Than when his friends *tripp'd* for the *Loan* ;
When all together by the ears,
They quarrell'd for the largeft fhares :
" *Trip up*, good lads ! the Statefman cries,
" Who wins—fhall have the greateft prize :
" No longer here attendance dance,
" For what is got is all a *chance :*
" Who can expect that I, the nation
" Can fave by dint of *fpeculation ?*
" The very Patriots advance,
" The nation muft be fav'd—by *chance:*
" But, good Sir GR-Y*, firft fhut the door,
" ('Tis what you've often done before)
" Left any fkulking *Whig* fhould whip in,
" And catch the minifter a *tripping*."—
Contending jobbers lik'd the plan,
Bankers and brokers to a man ;

---

* J-hn D-nn-ng, Efq. † Right Honble If--c B--rè, mem-
bers for Calne in Wilts.
‡ Right Honble Frd-r-ck, Lord N-rth, reprefentative for
Banbury, Oxon. PREMIER.
* Sir Gr-y C--p-r, Bart. member for Saltafh in Cornwall,
joint-Secretary to the Treafury, &c. &c.

No miniſter could more ſucceed,—
The *bulls* and *bears* were all agreed.—

Thus *oppoſition* would be quiet,
London ne'er know another riot,
Would GEORGE, grown partial to new faces,
Let Patriots·*trip up* for places:
For ſee! how many of them hanker
After the *Admiralty-anchor* * !
How many look with longing eye
On *England*'s lofty *Treaſury!*
Full many Courtier's head they'd lop,
Could they once get upon the top;
What numbers of them like thy pay,
And eke thy conſequence, Sir GR-Y:
How fain would men of ſtomachs nice,
From R-GBY's† pudding take a ſlice..
Ah! R-GBY's is a ſnug affair,
Full twenty-thouſand pounds a year!
With R-GBY all would take a cup,
Could they but get him to *trip up*;
Or for a *tit-bit* ſlily hitch in
With T-LB-T ‡ in the royal kitchen.

'Tis now full twenty years or more,
Old Whigs have bled at ev'ry pore;

* Seal of office of the Firſt Lord of the Admiralty.
† Right Honble. R-ch--d R-gby, repreſentative for Tavi-
ſtock, Devon; Paymaſter-general of his Majeſty's forces,
&c. &c.
‡ Right Honble, Earl T-lb-t, Lord Steward of the Houſe-
hold, &c.

Doom'd

Doom'd in all counties thro' the nation,
To an unnat'ral *Scotch flarvation.*
Lord ADV-C-TE* extols the lot,—
Such is the mildnefs of a Scot :
In vain *old honeſt Whigs* petition,
Lamenting *Britain*'s loft condition,
Her tarnifh'd luftre, faded glory,
The triumphs of the *white-ros'd Tory :*
In vain prefer their loyal fuit,
And curfe the influence of B-TE†,
Who fills all pofts for private ends,
And calls his *creatures*—" *The King's friends.*"
But not a foul of them can flip in,
For N-RTH is now grown deaf to *tripping.*

The India Company behold
Rich *Nabobs*—trembling for their gold !
Directors lending each a hand
To fave their *territorial* land !
How like Sir H-GH ‡ they *knot* and *fplice ?*
All had been ended in a trice,
Had but the Knight in the *blue garter*
Tripp'd up with them for a NEW CHARTER.

How foon would civil difcord ceafe;
How foon our broils be hufh'd in peace ;
State-matters all meet calm decifion,
The *Houfe* ne'er hear of a *divifion.*

---

* Right Honble H-nry D-nd-s, Lord Advocate of Scotland, member for Edinburgh-fhire.

† Right Honble J-hn St--rt, Earl of B-te.—" *Bleſſed be the peace makers!*"

‡ *The Governor of Greenwich Hofpital.*

When

When that the *Speaker* puts the *queſtion*
On *motions* of a hard digeſtion ;
Would F-x and B--RE, B-RKE and D-NN-NG,
And men of parts, and men of cunning,
Diſmiſſing *patriotic* fury,
Act, like—the *N-rf-lk* TRIPPING JURY ?

THIS is, in every ſenſe, a jumble of political
traits, too vague and diſſolutary to demand
ſerious attention. With regard to the circumſtance of a JURY *tripping up* for a verdict, which
our hero avers to be *a fact*, we do not ſee
why Mr. C-ke and Sir H— H-- ſhould be ſo
unmercifully *tripped.* The PUBLIC were in full
poſſeſſion of the diſpute agitated by *appeal,* and
conſequently the proper *jury* to determine on its
merits ; though it required not the *toſſing up of*
a ſhilling to return the verdict, unanimouſly, *felo-*
de-ſe. This freſh attack on their character as
gentlemen and men of honor, is an inſult to the
jury, which DICK had, of his own choice, im-
paneled. An appeal to the *public* is a matter of
ſerious conſideration, and ought not to be given
too raſhly :—but there is no appeal from their
deciſion in literary ſuits. Prejudices are eaſily
received, but not ſo eaſily removed; and all the
ſophiſtry and innumerable *minutiæ* of the ableſt
writers, *en advocatus,* will fail in effect : and, by
endeavouring to prove *too much*—prove *nothing*
at all ! " He that is too much a huckſter, often
" loſes a bargain; as he that is too little ſo,
" often

" often purchafes a law-fuit," is an excellent American maxim, as confonant on this fide of the Atlantic as on the other, and perfectly fo with Mr. MERRY-FELLOW, throughout life.

DICK is here found *tripping* with minifters of ftate, and with grooms of the Augean ftable. Patriots *tripping* up the heels of tripping minifters, and tripping minifters *tripping* up for the loaves and fifhes, whilft the * * * * and his people are *tripping*—in the literal fenfe of the word : and the belligerent powers are *tripping up*—for the dominion of this devoted country !

— — — BRITAIN, alas ! how chang'd,
How fallen from that envy'd height !— —

LYTT.

By a feries of meafures, erroneous and impolitic, hath not thefe kingdoms been plunged, from the very pinnacle of human greatnefs, into an abyfs of wretchednefs ? 'Tis now too late to recover what we have loft ! but it is not too late to punifh the author of our ruin ! fhould the proof come home to an individual :

" Without one fneaking virtue in thy train,
" O precious villain ! fcoundrel ! rogue in grain !

IT is a tribute to his country—to juftice—to heaven ! Millions of money and thoufands of
lives

lives have been facrificed to accomplifh—what? why the ruin of our trade! the difgrace of our arms! and the lofs of dominion!—Our feelings as men, as liege fubjects, prompt us to thefe bitter reflections. AMERICA loft! France triumphant! Spain rampant, Holland en paffant, and all the world in their fober fenfes—but poor Old England! DISPATCH, the life of bufinefs, and the foul of war, was never exerted more fuccefsfully than in the Mauritanian work done by the Gorgon knot of evil councilors towards the ruin of this country. To lofe in feven years what we have been acquiring for ages! O Fortune! Fortune! thou art a jilt; or elfe, our fins are equal to the meafure of our woes.

SAVE us, O Lord! for we are finking, faith the Pfalmift; and may we, by a yet timely reforma▾ tion, feek thy hand to crufh our enemies?

———————dii vifa fecundant.   Luc.

Profper the vifion, heav'n!

Ejaculations of prayer, when offered with fincerity, will, we truft, be received by the Almighty difpenfer of the world, with benignity and regard. O! may the ftubborn hearts of thofe who advifed and fupported coerfive meafures, as the means of conciliating the minds of men, be turned, and may they humble themfelves

felves before God. The ingenious Dr. Prieſtley
hath this paſſage ; " What torrents of human
" blood has the reſtleſs ambition of mortals
" ſhed, and in what complicated diſtreſs has
" the diſcontent of powerful individuals involved
" a great part of their ſpecies!" but to leave
this gloomy ſubjeƈt, and return to DICK MERRY-
FELLOW, who we left *tripping* with the national
jury, within a *few days* of being *tripped up* by the
grim tyrant, Death, *ſans ceremonie.*

" Seiz'd with ſuch whims, with frenzy ſo diverting,
" Cruel ! to cloſe the ſcene, and drop the curtain."

AFTER a life, *rota fortuna, ſic*, ſpent in the extremes of good and bad fortune, and after being
forely afflicted with the gout for ninety-five
weeks, he departed this life, on Friday the four-
teenth of September, 1781, at Mount-Amelia
in the county of Norfolk, aged fifty-eight years.
He is gone to receive his reward in heaven,
where neither moth nor ruſt doth corrupt, and where
thieves break not thorough and ſteal.

HE was interred in the north iſle of Ingoldiſ-
thorpe church, oppoſite the north door : an old
ſtone was taken up, where he lies buried, and laid
down afterwards, with only RICHARD GARDINER,
Esq. on it, though a handſome mural monu-
                                                              ment

ment is intended to be put up with a suitable infcription *.

> —— *Poſt cineres gloria ſera venit.* MART.
> Fame to our aſhes comes, alas ! too late ;
> And praiſe ſmells rank upon the coffin-plate.

From the *Norwich Mercury* of Saturday, October 6, 1781, we extract the following, inferted in that paper by defire of the gentleman who fent it to the printer.

" The late Major Gardiner wrote the follow-
" ing lines, which he particularly requeſted of
" his executor, might be engraved on his tomb,—
" The tomb was laſt Saturday erected, with the
" defired infcription.

" RICHARD GARDINER, Efq. died September 14,
1781, in the 58th year of his age.
" The man befet with ev'ry earthly woe ;
" Whoſe boſom-friend turns out his deadly foe ;
" Whoſe mind's diftracted with corroding care ;
" Whoſe body's rack'd beyond his pow'r to bear ;
" Whoſe wife and children bear imperious ſway,
" O'er him they ought to cheriſh and obey :
" Where one man meets with all thefe ills combin'd,
" The grave's the only refuge fuch a wretch can find.
R. G."

" * I had my failings, be the truth confefs'd ;
" And, reader, can'ft thou boaſt a blamelefs breaſt ?

SINCE the above appeared in the Norwich papers, we are credibly informed, that no such EPITAPH was put on his tomb-stone, yet it is not so well afcertained, that he did *not write it.* Be that as it may, fome credit is due to the veracity of the lines, which, we are forry to fay, bear too ftrong a femblance of his temporal affairs.

From the Norfolk Chronicle, October, 13, 1781.

" Verfes wrote on reading an Epitpah in the
" Norwich Mercury, *falfely* and *malicioufly* af-
" ferted to be penn'd and engraved on the
" tomb of the late Major GARDINER of
" Mount-Amelia in Norfolk.

" When Priam's fon, great Hector, nobly bled,
" The Grecian * hoft furround the hero dead :
" Safe from the arm, which hurl'd deftruction round,
" O poor revenge! they give each limb a wound.
" Not fo, when living, Hector mow'd his way
" Through their thinn'd legion, to the clofe of day.

* " When Hector was killed, fome of thofe daftard Greeks,
" who were afraid to face him when alive, covered his dead
" body with wounds, to fatisfy their revenge.

Vide HOM. ILLIAD."

" But

. " But fay, mean herd, the body fpoil'd of breath;
" Muft malice live, beyond the hour of death ?
" The dead are facred ; let revilings ceafe,
" And GARD'NER's.fhade with Hector's,—reft in peace

THUS lived, and thus died, DICK MERRY-
FELLOW, of ferious and facetious memory !

What is this life, that mortals idly crave?
The noify paffport to the filent grave.

A man, who, according to the character given of
him in our title-page, had

Learning to inftruct, wit to entertain,
To moralize with eafe, and fatirize with pain.

IN taking a review of thefe memoirs, we find,
that we have anticipated, by curfory remarks,
thofe reflections which generally arife after the
deceafe of a perfon, whofe life and converfation
was intimately known to us. *Shakefpeare* hath
beautifully defcribed the ages of man, in the play
of As YOU LIKE IT ! and *Horace*, by the following elegant line :

Ætatis cujufque netandi funt tibi mores.

What foibles wait on life through ev'ry ftage !
Our youth a wild-fire, and a froft our age !

THE eccentricity of our hero's genius rendered
him an exception to the general rule of life
laid

laid down by writers, who draw us "*not* what
we are, but what we ought to be." The plain
duties of morality, which ought to govern our
actions, are too circumfcribed for the man of
fafhion, or the flave of wit; and thofe beings
who move in the circle of the *beau monde,* are
as ignorant of Mr. Pope's *multum in parva,* as
he whofe ill-placed vivacity, gets the better of his
good manners.

> " A *wit's* a feather, and a *chief's* a rod,
> " An HONEST MAN's the nobleft work of God!

Is genius to be confidered as a natural gift, or
an effect of education? and are men of a certain
turn of mind cenfurable for thofe follies which
rafhnefs and impetuofity hurries them into, and
which is as difficult to account for, as to reftrain.
A certain noble Earl, of an open generous heart,
who on all occafions, whether acting in the
quality of *fenator, ftatefman, ambaffador,* or at the
head of *armies,* was ever diftinguifhed for his
coolnefs and equal temper, but at WHIST was
occafionally fo ruffled, and became fo touchy, that
he has been known to quarrel even with *women,*
if the cards went againft him;—in other refpects,
the beft bred man alive! DICK MERRY-FELLOW
was a man of quick feelings, and of a temper
rather hafty and paffionate: the warmth of his difpofition, and his nice fenfibility of honor, involved
him frequently in broils, which he would readily
vindicate

vindicate, either by the *pen* or the *fword.* If the feverity of the former could not procure a con-ceffion, nor provoke a retaliation, he would then have recourfe to the latter; as in the cafe of Sir H. H. and Mr. C. Speaking of this matter to a friend, fometime before his death, he declared, that " in heat at firft, and in refentment for ex-
" treme ill ufage, I wrote thofe LETTERS, neither
" of which would ever have been publifhed, but
" for the outrageous and unmerited infult I re-
" ceived from Mr. C. and which, in vindication
" of my own *honor,* I was under a neceffity of
" doing, but might have been eafily prevented
" by the leaft conceffion that had been made,
" and which I had a right to expect, and till it
" is done, fhall think myfelf at liberty to be as
" *free* with their characters as I pleafe, and I
" fhall of courfe expofe them *to the public* upon
" every occafion that offers. I wrote Mr. C.
" word, " continued our hero," very lately, *that if*
" *he was offended at my paft publications, or fhould be*
" *at any future ones, I fhould be ready to give him fatis-*
" *faction whenever he called upon me, and without ac-*
" *quainting a third perfon, like that poltron his friend*
" *Sir H.*"

I T will not, we hope, be thought invidious, or too minute, to mention, that *Mount-Amelia* had been, for fometime before Mr. MERRY-FEL-LOW's deceafe, advertifed for public fale. Mrs.
G.

G. her daughter and younger son, quitted the
premifes on Sunday, Oct. 14, and, on the Wednefday following, the houfehold-furniture, &c.
were fold by auction for the benefit of creditors.
There being no executor of his will, Mrs. G. refufed to take upon her the adminiftration, for fear
of being brought into trouble, as his debts far
exceeded his effects. The houfe and land, we
are alfo told, is taken by the mortgagee; and
thus is the remains of our hero's terreftrious
affairs difperfed! He, who had fhone in all the
majefty of *print*; who had influence *on paper* to
affect the choice of reprefentatives in parliament; who had *feen* the beft company, and had
rolled in his own carriage;—whofe abilities were
the terror and admiration of all!

" His faults, or virtues, who can juftly tell?
" No mortal higher foar'd, nor lower fell.

DICK abhorred the trite maxim of Charles II.
" *Court your enemies, and your friends will be your*
" *friends ftill.* This infamous principle," fays
he, " which has frequently prevailed in latter
" times, has been found (and always will when-
" ever purfued) to do equal mifchief in public as
" in private life."—This is very well in theory,
Mr. MERRY-FELLOW, but no one ever *experienced*
its inefficacy in practice more than yourfelf!
for, had you had temper to fhew lefs of your wit

and more of your prudence, you had not been
" the fport of fortune, nor the butt of fools !"
He that lives in a houfe of glafs, fays the proverb,
fhould not be the firft to throw ftones : yet no timid
confideration ever deterred him from *kicking
againft the pricks.* Rather too confident of his
" fcale of talents," our hero cared not by whom,
or in what manner, he was attacked. To treat
him *de haut en bas,* or prefume on the fanction of
wealth or *power* to awe him, he would anfwer, in
the words of HORACE, *melius non tangere clamo.*

> Peace is my delight, not FLEURY's more,'.
> But *touch* me, and no minifter fo *fore*;
> Whoe'er offends, at fome unlucky time,
> Slides into verfe, and hitches in a rhime,
> Sacred to ridicule his whole life long,
> And the *fad* burthen of fome *merry* fong.
>
> POPE.

HE always thought himfelf of more confequence than he really was, and would readily
become a party in an affair from which he could
derive neither reputation nor pecuniary profit.

> " Who meddle thus with other's cares,
> " Too oft neglect their own affairs :
> " But who abroad for bufinefs roam,
> " Should nothing leave undone at home.

HE would have made an admirable civilian,
for he could defend as ftrenuoufly as he could
condemn—

condemn—the fame caufe: and though often directed and warped by prejudice, yet he ftudi-oufly kept up appearances, by plaufibility of rea-foning : or, in other words—*out of the law.* Though he duly reverenced legal authority, he difpifed the *infolence* of office; and would fre-quently lament, that " There *was* a time when true diftinction was held to be as VIRTUE only :

—Nobilitas fola eſt atque unica virtus.

THAT truly noble fentiment, *non bene vivere, non eſt,* " Not to live well, is not to live at all," he held as the brighteft gem of moral philo-fophy, but few men ever miftook the means of acquiring it more than our hero. His attach-ments were ftrong, (wou'd we could fay they were inviolable) as were his refentments. His generofity was fuperior to his circumftances, and his zeal to ferve was free from referve, or reftric-tion. He who wifhes to be feared is feldom be-loved ; as fuch, DICK was oftener flattered than admired.

IF DICK had a friend or two who tickled his imagination, by a partial adherence to his rea-foning, or by giving an affirmative to his com-plaints of ill-ufage from others, he would receive the fingle inftance of tenacity, as a full and fufficient teftimony—that *every body* thought fo.

What

What ev'ry body fays, is often true;
But very often 'tis a falfhood too:

Or, according to HORACE, *Interdum vulgus rectum videt*; *eft*, *ubi peccat*. If e'er he out-ftep'd the modefty of nature, or raifed merriment or wonder by the violation of truth, he difdained to retreat, and could never be brought to ac-knowledge an error—either in judgment or of the heart, though frequently warned of the dan-ger of purfuing a wrong impulfe.

HE was a man of ftrong natural parts, highly cultivated by education and company : his learn-ing was great, his reading and experience ex-tenfive, and his memory retentive : his imagi-nation was quick, and his judgment folid. As his own feelings were the moft fenfitive fo was he a perfect mafter of the paffions of others; and although intolerably impatient of infult, he was always on his guard, and kept within the pale of the *law*. The flighteft appearance of neglect or injury would roufe him ; but, like the lion, his refentment would, on proper con-ceffion, as quickly fubfide ; and the moft cordial reconciliation immediately fucceed the moft in-veterate calumny,—and fo *vice verfa*.

IF DICK was not quite a *merry* fellow he was by no means a *forry* fellow ; and whilft he com-plained of the wheel of fortune, " now up, now " down,"

" down," he willingly acknowledged frailties
and faults in common with other men.   .

— Vitijs nemo fine nafcitur optimus ille
Qui minimis urgetur——

In converfation, he was brilliant and copious;
his addrefs eafy and polite. If the meafure of
his wit was *leeky* at both ends (for what came in
at the one went as profufely out at the other)
he had, as it were, an inexhauftible fource of humor, given with a degree of *vis comica,* affumed
fo naturally, and worn fo eafily, that while it
rendered the fatire peculiarly pleafant, it eftablifhed its truth, and gave it irrefiftible force : but,
as a fuperficial knowledge in fcience makes men
pedantic, and a fmattering in law renders them
litigious, fo an habituation in wit turns men
into buffoons :—this is what the moderns call—
a *bore.*

His figure and appearance was that of the
gentleman,—though not genteel; being corpulent
and round-fhouldered. Whatever emotions of
difguft his rancor, and mal-apro-pos remarks
on the actions of *worthy* characters, might infpire, we could not look on him but with refpect and awe : his filver locks at once thawed
our refentment into reverence for his years, and
regard for his abilities. In effect, as beholding

" Wifdom

" Wifdom with periwigs,.with-caffocks grace,
" Courage with fwords, gentility with lace."

In his writings alfo, he was what naturalifts
call a *non-defcript:* at once ferious and comic;—
the lampoon, or the eulogium;—declamation
or clofe reafoning;—the flights of fancy or dull
epifode;—fententious and elaborate;—the *jeu-
d'efprit,* the fong, the epitaph, the *double en tendre,*
the epigram, the heroic, the Hudibraftic, rhap-
fodical queries, and unintelligible dogmas, are
all and each difcoverable in his writings.

— —*Inopem me copia fecit.*   Ovid.

— —Too much plenty makes me die for want.

ADDISON.

It would require the verbofity of a *Lexiphanes*
to exemplify the many beauties and enormities
that tiffue our heroe's LIFE and WRITINGS; it
muft not, therefore, be expected, that *we* can do
juftice to fo wide a text. Like the great eater
of *Wirtemberg* in Germany, who fwallowed a
block-tin ftandifh, with the pens, pen-knife, ink,
fand, and every thing it contained, DICK feemed
to poffefs the *requifites,* if not the genius, of an
author. His *coup d'effai* (page 10 of this memoir)
is a ftrong prefage of future excellence, but we
do not believe he ever *ftudied—to be an* AUTHOR,
nor held the opinion of the poet, who fays,

I not

I not for vulgar admiration write ;
To be *well* read, not *much*, is my delight.

His thoughts were generally thrown together
without much order, and inftead of a regular
progrefs from one truth to another, we only fee
the wild fallies of a vigorous mind, frequently
returning in the fame circle, and fometimes running quite out of fight, with the eccentric ra-
pidity of a comet. His allufions were, however, truly claffical, and his high-flown metaphors and compound epithets were peculiarly
happy. Had he purfued the *Belles-lettres* fyfte-
matically, his luxuriancy of thought and folid
acquaintance with the claffics would have rendered him confpicuous among the literati, and
his lines, what is now a rarity,

——Verses written by a POET !

Satire was his grand *forte*; and to this he
was ftimulated by that levity of temper and in-
fatiate difpofition which deftroyed the very exiftence of plaufibility. " 'Tis a peculiar happi-
" nefs of the times, when a man may think as
" he pleafes, and fpeak as he thinks," fays
Tacitus ; but this confcientious liberty ought not
to be proftituted to licentious purpofes, nor exercifed by bards, who

——— All agree,
" Damn'd's the fuperlative degree !"

R 4   It

IT is not difficult, even for men of the loweſt
capacity, to perplex the faireſt reaſoner, by
doubts and objections; and much leſs ſo for a
man of wit and words, like our hero, to repre-
ſent the ſoundeſt argument in a light ludicrous
enough to make it ſeem ridiculous: but it ſhould
be remembered, that it is much eaſier to laugh
at the beſt ſyſtem, than to form one of the worſt!
To unmaſk hypocriſy, and to correct vice, is,
indeed, to be highly uſeful: The ſharp pen of
Aretin once made moſt of the ſovereign princes
of Europe his tributaries; and the keen *Iambics*
of *Archilochus* and *Hipponax*, are ſaid to have
driven the perſons, who were the ſubjects of them,
to ſuch acts of deſperation, as to hang and
drown themſelves:—we believe no writer of the
preſent age can produce ſo tragical an effect as
the Greek poet, whoſe ſatirical works were forbid to be read by the Spartans; ſo highly ſea-
ſoned were they by the ſalt of Parnaſſus,

DICK's ſatire was poignant, but not always
juſt. In his *Juvenalian* lines, the poetic *furor*
would hurry him into the moſt violent invective,
and low humor: every little incident was
wrought up in the web of defamation, for,

    Triumphant, malice rag'd thro' private life:
                                              POPE.

And all ties of former friendſhip were ſacrificed
to the preſent moment of feelings. " Tremble,
                                              " thou

" thou wretch ! that haft within thee undivulged
" crimes, unwhipt of juftice !"

Qui capit, ille fecit.

WE have often regreted, that Mr. MERRY-
FELLOW never engaged his talents in dramatic
writing, for which, according to our ideas, he
feems better fuited than one half of the modern
play-wrights : for though there is a tirefome
famenefs in the manner of drawing his characters, yet they are, in general, nervoufly and
ftrickingly expreffed, and fhew his great acquaintance both with men and books. *Butler*
has very juftly defcribed the *minor* poets in the
following four lines.

—Thofe who write in rhime ftill make
The one verfe for the other's fake;
For, one for *fenfe*, and one for *rhyme*,
I think's fufficient at one time.   H U D.

As confiftency formed no part of DICK's
charafter, if we except that permanent infatuation that guided all his aftions, like the

" —— —— Man who knows the *right*
" Yet does the *wrong*—with all his might.

Inconfiftency may appear, even in this our opinion of him, but we fpeak to his *memoirs* as
they really occurred, and not as they *might* be :
and we have, throughout the compilation, endeavoured

voured rather to draw a veil over thofe foibles which marked the contour of his life, than expofe human frailties :—as he had vices fo had he virtues :

Nemo vitijs fine nafcitur, optimus ille,
Qui minimis urgetur.——

Adopting his own maxim, when applied to by a friend to re-publifh fome of his felect compofitions, " I war not with the dead."

———— *ceffit furor, et rabida ora quierunt.*
VIRG.

Ceas'd is his fury, and he foams no more.

DRAWING near, as we are, *to the End of the Chapter of Accidents*, we recommend thefe lines to our courteous reader ;—

" Juftice fhould weigh impartial in her fcales,
" As *folly* triumphs, or as *fenfe* prevails.

And, as DICK MERRY-FELLOW was, notwithftanding, friendly and humane, we hope he has found a peaceful afylum in heaven.

—— *Illa fe jactet in Aula.*   VIRGIL.
—— There let him reign.   DRYDEN.

ADDENDA.

ADDENDA.

ACADEMIE.

A D D E N D A.

AT the bottom of an advertiſement of "The *Tripping-Jury*, or an Eſſay on *Portraits* in Norfolk," in the Cambridge Chronicle of September 1, 1781.

"Where may be had, juſt publiſhed,

" The Bonfire of But-lands; or, The Humours of Wells:

" A New Norfolk Ballad.

" On the occaſion of a late trial at the affizes at Norwich.

" *Jamque Faces et Saxa Volant.*

Virg."

A

A printed copy of this Ballad hath not fallen
into our hands, but we have taken it from
an authentic manufcript.

To the tune of " the Archbifhop of Canterbury."

I SING, the time not long ago,
⠀⠀The city of W-LLS grew mad, Sir!
And frantic ran to TH-RSF-RᴀHall,
⠀⠀To take advice of CH-D, Sir!
The Doctor, never averfe to *fees*,
⠀⠀Cry'd! O ! *relief* is fure,
" *Salt water*, gentlemen, you want,
⠀⠀" It is a *certain cure*."
⠀⠀⠀⠀⠀⠀⠀⠀*Tol-de-rol-lol*, &c. &c.

But when returning home again
⠀⠀To W-LLS, they caft their eye, Sir!
The corporation, in amaze,
⠀⠀Beheld their *harbour* dry, Sir!
What could they do, for *Folks* relate
⠀⠀There was no *water* for them,
For *falt* and *frefh*, and tides and all,
⠀⠀Had been ftop't up at W-RH-M.
⠀⠀⠀⠀⠀⠀⠀⠀*Tol-de-rol-lol*, &c. &c.

To NORWICH for *noftrums* then they ran,
⠀⠀To get their *water* back, Sir!
There all the *faculty* declar'd—
⠀⠀That CH-D was but a *quack*, Sir!
They turn'd o'er ev'ry leaf to be found
⠀⠀In England's difpenfary,
But Doctor *Selden*,—death to their nofes,
⠀⠀Prefcribed a—*claufum mare !*
⠀⠀⠀⠀⠀⠀⠀⠀*Tol-de-rol-lol*, &c. &c.
⠀⠀⠀⠀⠀⠀⠀⠀⠀⠀⠀⠀And

And now the *fever* in their blood,
    Rag'd higher ftill and higher;
And finding no *water* could be got,
    They had recourfe to *fire*:
A gun fhot up to the chimney's top,
    They knew all *flames* would fmother;
For *fire* and *fire*, like nail and nail,
    Will drive out one another.

                Tol-de-rol-lol, &c. &c.

Then ftrait two *men of fenfe* they feiz'd,
    (There were but *two* in town, Sir!)
And tying them faft to BUTTER-FIELDS,
    To burn them hurried down, Sir!
In vain, for fuch CH-D-dian rage,
    'Tis heav'n only, quells, Sir!
And fo, the Lord have mercy now
    Upon the city of W-lls, Sir!

                Tol-de-rol-lol, &c. &c.

Printed for *Johnny Gig.*
    Auguft 3, 1781.

INTELLIGENCE EXTRAORDINARY.

(From the *Conteft*, December 26, 1767.)

WE hear from *Dublin*, that a noble *Lord*, famous
for his fkill in *caricaturas*, at a late public dinner
at his apartments, *took off* a gentleman a little remarkable
in his features: it happened that this gentleman was as
great a proficient in *caracaturas* as his *lordfhip*; and obferving, at the bottom of a long table, what he was about,
                                        took

took out his pencil alfo, and, on the back of a letter, drew a ftrong and very ridiculous likenefs of the noble *peer*, in the attitude of drawing. The latter, having finifhed his own performance, handed it down the table, till it came to the gentleman himfelf, who, laughing heartily at it, flip'd into his neighbour's hand his own *caricatura* of my *lord*, and paffed it up the table on the other fide. A general laugh enfued, and the noble *peer* enjoying this public approbation of his humor, fat highly delighted, and in great fpirits ; when, in his turn, he was prefented with his own ridiculous figure, which had equally diverted half the company.—This unexpected ftroke vifibly made its impreffion ; he appeared much chagrin'd, and foon after retired, to the no fmall entertainment of the company, and indeed of the whole city, when the ftory was related in all its circumftances the following day.

From the Morning Herald, 1781.

A N E C D O T E S

Of the late Right Honorable *Charles Townfhend.*

IT was a very fingular circumftance that fhewed the effect of habit in this celebrated orator : he had been ufed to fpeak fo much in the Houfe of Commons *on his legs*, that he could never make the femblance of a fpeech, further than a few words, or a repartee, while fitting. When the principal merchants of London waited on him upon a great commercial regulation, he heard all they had to fay, and then, to anfwer them, rofe from his chair, faying, " I muft be on my legs, or I cannot fpeak to you at all."

His

His convivial wit at table (perhaps the moſt brilliant part of his charaĉter) was perpetual, varied, and aroſe
from trifles ſo minute, that he never wanted a perennial
fund; nor was he ſatisfied with the tribute of laughter
from thoſe at table with him, if all the footmen in the
room were not upon the broad grin; and he aĉtually
made Lady *Dalkeith*, part with a favorite footman of her
own, becauſe he had ſeveral times obſerved him with un-
moved muſcles, when the reſt could not reſtrain the riſi-
ble impulſe; his memory was prodigious, he never read
the claſſics, he had them all at his fingers ends from the
acquiſitions he had made at ſchool ; and that this is probable, appears from a circumſtance that happened at
Rainham, where his brother, George, the preſent Lord,
loſt twenty guineas in a bett to him, that he did not
know what was in an old leaſe, which George knew he
could have ſeen but *once* in his life ; Charles repeated
every clauſe, and every circumſtance with ſuch exaĉtneſs,
that the whole family were aſtoniſhed. His talents,
with all their powers, had ſhades that were unaccount-
able, unleſs we attribute them to timidity ; he had his
hours when he could do nothing, and he avoided the
Houſe; when he knew he ſhould meet with a violent
and prepared oppoſition, he then had his political cholics,
a real diſtemper indeed, but ſo often feigned that at laſt
he was not believed, and he died—for want of a phyſician!

S   The

The following STANZAS were wrote and sent to the Right Honorable the Earl of Orford, by RICHARD GARDINER, Efq. of *Mount-Amelia,* on his Lordfhip's birth-day, April 13th, foon after he had recovered from a dangerous fit of illnefs.

To the EARL *of* ORFORD.

H O W eager is the thirft of fame,
    How few that e'er attain it!
How oft by folly lofe the prize
    As quickly as they gain it!

In *fifty-nine* with envy feen
    Was PITT's meridian glory:
In *fixty-one* CHATHAM became
    The jeft of ev'ry Tory.

So anxious for their future fame
    (How all men wifh to know it)
Deceiv'd, till death fhall clofe the fcene,
    By flatt'rer, or by poet!

To you, Lord ORFORD, tho' 'tis rare,
    The boon by fate was giv'n,
Your real friends and future fame
    To know on this fide heav'n:

Lamented as you were by all,
    'Tis pleafing now to hear it,
The laurel of the grave you've won,
    And more——you live to wear it.

From

From the Cambridge Chronicle of June 30, 1781.

THE *hymenæal* torch never flamed with greater bright-
nefs than at prefent in the meridian of *Hull:* we
hear the *weſtern* battalion of the NORFOLK militia are
held in high efteem by the northern ladies, particularly
the *widows*, ever allowed to be the beft judges of *connubial*
accomplifhments. Three grenadiers ferving for the
hundreds of LAUNDITCH and MITFORD have, within
this fortnight, offered up their vows at the altar of *Hymen*,
leading in three buxom and prolific reliċts, two of them
mothers of feven, and the third of eleven beautiful babes,
—a noble encreafe to the declining population in Norfolk,
and to which thefe weftern fons of gallantry are likely to
contribute greatly, as the laft accounts from the corps
bring advice that more widows were daily coming in, all
bleffed with a happy and numerous progeny. The *favors*
worn by the grenadier company on the occafion of thefe
aufpicious nuptials had, wrought in gold and filver,

Pulchrâ facias te prole parentem,.

The brides and bridegrooms, with a *fuite* of twenty-five
fine fubjeċts for colonization, croffed the Humber laft Monday, by permiffion of the commanding officer, to make the
tour of Norfolk, where the ladies and their beautiful
branches of *olive* are to be planted during the operations of
the prefent war.

The purport of the above paragraph had no
foundation in truth, but was wrote by DICK, in
a merry mood, only to alarm the juftices, about
providing fettlements for the wives and children
of militia-men.

S 2   EPITAPH

EPITAPH on a grave-ftone put down in 1778, to
the memory of Mr. William Moncy, farmer
and tenant at Weft-Rudham in Norfolk, to
Lord Vifcount Townfhend, his father, and
grandfather:

Written by RICHARD GARDINER, Efq.

TITLES and trophies deck the ftatefman's grave,
And pompous tombs immortalize the brave;
Yet rural virtue finds the road to fame,
And boafts no titles—but an honeft name.
A plain good man lies here—Herald's fay more,
Who ufher pageants at the abbey-door!
The path of honefty WILL. MONEY trod:
" An honeft man's the nobleft work of God."
Vain epitaphs the author's genius fhow,
While all is duft, mere duft, that lies below:
'Tis all mere duft!—the reft the poet's wit,
Or whether 'tis WILL. MONEY—or WILL. PITT.

THE following VERSES were infcribed to the
memory of Mrs. HOSTE of Ingoldifthorpe in
Norfolk, who died in 1775, much lamented, by
Richard Gardiner Efq; " Mrs. Hofte was a moft
" amiable woman, and efteemed by all who knew
" her: perfectly well bred; eafy and chearful in
" her converfation, though of a weak and very
" fluctuating ftate of health; of an open generous
" heart;

[261]

" heart: fincere and fteady in her friendfhips: in
" her carriage uniformly pleafing, and in her drefs
" the *fimplex munditijs* of Horace,—inexpreffibly
" neat."

L ONG in affliction, long in ficknefs tried,
  Calm and ferene the patient parent died:
In all the duties of domeftic life,
The tender mother, and the careful wife:
O early loft!—let maufoleums boaft,
A name more honor'd than the name of HOSTE!

Peace to thy afhes, lady! may thy grave
No ftorms affail, nor hoarfe refounding wave;
But " angels fing a requiem to thy foul,"
Till light'nings fcorch and whirlwinds fhake the pole;
Till the laft trump, re-echoing thro' the fkies,
In awful fummons calls the dead to rife!
Then heav'n fhall ope its everlafting door,
And pain and forrow be thy lot no more.

———————

TRANSLATION of a Latin Epitaph to the memory
of Thomas Gurlin, Efq. who died Auguft 3,
1644, and lies buried in the parifh church of
Snettifham in Norfolk:

By RICHARD GARDINER, Efq.

STRANGER! beneath this tomb, in hope to rife,
A man of wifdom and of virtue lies.
Thrice *mayor* of Lynn, and *member* thrice he fat:
Thrice England's Commons in full fenate met:

Firm

Firm and unfhaken in his country's eaufe;
Bold to defend its liberty and laws.

Such GURLIN was! no contraƈt, bribe, or plaċe,
E'er drew upon his honeft vote difgrace.
Read, venal members, as you pafs along,
And envy virtue, which you cannot wrong.

And thou, brave ftranger! whofoe'er thou art,
Shouldft thou condemn him, aƈt a nobler part.
Now that his virtues fleep in peaceful reft,
To rifing ftorms oppofe a firmer breaft:
The fhocks of time with manlier fpirit bear,
Then from his honor'd brow the laurels tear,
And LYNN fhall boaft her member and her mayor.

From the London Magazine of April, 1763.

ADDRESS from a certain CITY.

PLUMP'D up with plumb-pudding, plumb-dumpling,
    and porridge,
We your M-j-fty's *Mayor, Court,* and *Commons* of *Norwich,*
In our notions of LIBERTY never miftaken,
And " firm as your M-j-fty's virtues unfhaken"*,
Return you our thanks—by our friend Mr. B. c-n :
Our thanks for a PEACE—now your arms are viƈtorious,
As lafting and fafe—as 'tis happy and glorioust.

---

   * *Vide* Addrefs before the preliminaries.
       † *Ditto.*

I N·

INSCRIPTION to the memory of Francis Longe,
Efq. of Spixworth in Norfolk, who died in
1776; and to his lady, *obijt* 1760.

TO the proud prince let *maufoleums* rife,
And cloud-capt *pyramids* infult the fkies!
There ftate-entomb'd magnificently lie,
Kings and their queens,—for kings and queens muft die !
Friendfhip and beauty, this fond pair afleep,
O'er the fad fhrine eternal vigils keep !
All focial virtues blefs'd the heart of LONGE,
Whilft his fair confort charm'd th' admiring throng :
No arch we bend, no tow'ring column rear,
Love, truth, and honor, are the heralds here.

THE 28th ariticle of the Monthly Catalogue,
in the MONTHLY REVIEW for April, 1754, is
" *A letter to* John Shadwell, *Efq.* of the county
" of *Norfolk* ; with obfervations on the hiftory
" of PUDICA, and fome thoughts on a town
" and country life. By *Richard Merry-fellow,*
" Efq. 8vo. 6d. *Swan.*"

IN the fame month's REVIEW, is " *A Letter*
" *to the Honble.* George *Townfhend,* Knight of the
" fhire for the county of *Norfolk,* during the
" laft parliament, in anfwer to the *Norfolk Far-*
" *mer's fentiments,* &c. By *Richard Gardiner,*
" Efq. 8vo. 6d. *Swan.*—" A mere invective
" againft, but no anfwer to, the *Farmer's fen-*
" *timents.*"

THE

THE firſt of theſe publications we have feen, printed on thirty-four pages, dated April 10, but the latter has not fallen in our way. This. LETTER to Mr. *Shadwell*, contains little more than a recapitulation of what is to be met with in *the Hiſtory of* PUDICA, and ſome diſſolutary conſiderations, occaſioned by the death of the Right Honorable Henry Pelham; in which, many *charaɛters*, and a great deal of *reading* is diſ-played.

☞ ANY thing further, relative to DICK MERRY-FELLOW, which may hereafter be communicated to the publiſhers of this *Memoir*, will be thankfully received, and properly attended to, ſhould a *fecond* edition be found neceſſary.